Teach Yourself Animation Coding in Scratch 3
Second Edition
Copyright ©2021 by Achal

All rights reserved. No part of this book shall be reproduced, stored in a retrieval system, or transmitted by any means, electronic, mechanical, photocopying, recording, or otherwise, without written permission from the Author.

Trademarks
Scratch is a visual programming language developed by MIT Media Lab for coding animation. Use of the term in this book should not be regarded as affecting the validity of any trademark or service mark.

Warning and Disclaimer
Every effort has been made to make this book as complete and as accurate as possible, but no warranty or fitness is implied. The information provided is on an "as is" basis. The author and the publisher shall have neither liability nor responsibility to any person or entity concerning any loss or damages arising from the information contained in this book.

Note to Parents

Coding or programming from this book just requires a computer it can have any type of operating systems like Windows, Linux, or Mac. This book will help develop technical temperament, logical thinking, promote problem-solving skills, promote creativity. Even if your child chooses any other career than programming or computer science, the coding in this stage will help in the overall development and problem-solving skills.

The "scratch" is a block-based programming language developed by MIT Media Lab and can either be installed as a standalone application or can be run directly through your web browser. The programming language is for children aged 8 to 16, however, you can anyone can join scratch programming for entertainment and learning. Scratch allows users to make small animations, stories, play music, and develop small games.

I have read many responses of parents who are delighted that their child can code at the age of 6. In my opinion, do not force the child. Every child has a different taste. Some like to dance, play or sing and some like to create games or code. Some child develops logical brain late in their growth while some do it early. It is always suggested to encourage the child for logical reasoning by playing board games or fun games.

If your child is young and fails to understand the logic, do not compare or get panic. Give your child some more time to develop. Ask your child to take scratch as an entertaining tool and game and not as a coding course.

Keywords: scratch 3.0, scratch MIT, online scratch

Contents

Note to Parents 2

Contents 3

Chapter -1: The scratch platform 6
    The Scratch Platform 7
    The Sprites 8
    The Background 9
    The code blocks 10
    The code window 11
    Start/Stop Button 12
    Other parts of the scratch platform 13
    Assignment 14

Chapter-2: The Animated Birthday Card 15
    Setting the stage for animation 15
    The Costumes of Sprites 16
    Changing Costumes 18
    The Loops 20
    The Wait code block 21
    Say and Stop All Code Block 23
    Adding Sound/Music to the Animation 23

Chapter 3: Practice loop and movements 26
    Exploring pen extension 26
    Drawing using Pen 28
    Re-set sprite after each run 28
    Drawing a square on screen 30
    Drawing square with a loop 32
    Drawing pattern from a square 32
    Drawing letter "A" on screen 33
    Star Pattern 35
    Drawing Circle 36
    Pattern created from a Circle 36
    Assignment 38

Chapter 4: Giving motion to Sprites 39

    Goto Random Position 39

    Glide 40

    Move to x and y 40

    Dancing Girl project 41

Chapter 5: Pong Game (Ball Bouncing) 45

    Bouncing Ball from edge 45

    Moving the paddle 47

    Bouncing Ball from the paddle 49

    Understanding Direction 51

    Game end coding 54

    End Game Screen 55

    Broadcast Message 57

    Adding Score 59

    The Entire Code 61

Chapter-6: Simple Baseball Game 63

    Sprites Required 64

    Bowling 64

    Batsman's action 65

    Shot on ball 66

    Score Keeping 66

    The Entire Code 67

Chapter-7: Balloon Burst Game 68

    Required of Sprites 69

    Transparent image 69

    Searching transparent image on google images 69

    Adding an image as Costume 70

    Moving balloon randomly on the screen 71

    POP the Balloon 73

    Solving issues 74

    The Entire Code 75

Chapter-8: Balloon Bursting with Finger 76

    Video Sensing 76

    The Code 78

Chapter-9: Rocket Shooting Game (Medium Toughness) 80

    Step 1: Make wand moving 81

    Step 2: Shooting the lightning 82

    Step 3: Moving the rocket 85

    Step 4: A Blast on being hit 87

    Step 5: Counting Score 88

    Step 6: Counting Life 89

    Step 7: Difficulty Level: Increase Speed 90

    Step 8: Difficulty Level: Rocket movement to avoid the aim 90

    The complete code 91

Chapter 10: Text to speech 93

    Exploring code blocks for text to speech 93

    Implementation of text to speech 94

Solutions to Assignments 95

Chapter -1: The scratch platform

You can either download the scratch application on your computer for offline programming or can do online coding through your browser by visiting https://scratch.mit.edu/.

Scratch 3.0 can also be downloaded to your computer from **https://scratch.mit.edu/download** for windows computers. Scratch is also available for download for Linux users, but the version is old.

Here, I am using my web browser for coding, you can follow me to start with your first code. I have a chrome browser and I have opened the link "https://scratch.mit.edu/". You will have a window as shown below:

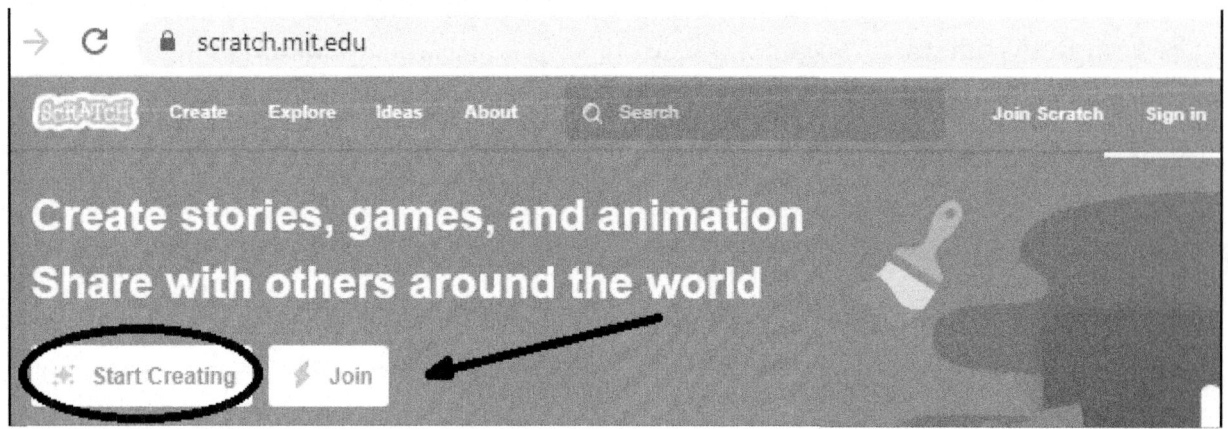

Click on "Start Creating" to get access to building blocks immediately, however, you won't be able to save your project. You can click "Join" to create an account on the scratch website. This will provide you some extra features on scratch like saving and sharing of projects.

For joining scratch you will need to choose a username and a password for yourself, make sure that you remember your username and password for future use. On the next page is the window to Join Scratch. This username and password can now be used any time to sign in and access the stuff that you made last time.

In case you have downloaded scratch 3.0 from its website and have installed it on your computer, there is no need to create an account on the scratch website.

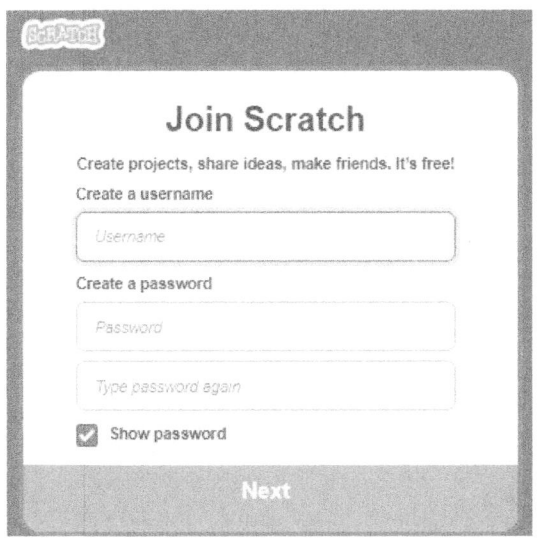 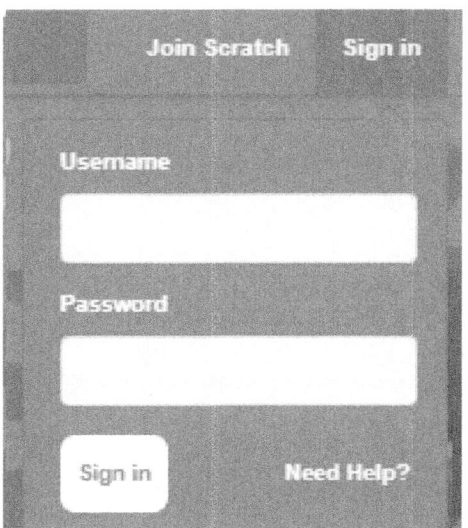

Now, sign in from the main page by providing the username and password you just choose. Click the sign-in button and you are in. The only benefit of sign-in as discussed earlier is that you can share your work with your friends or teachers and can save your work for future use and display.

The Scratch Platform

Now click on "create" to access your set of building blocks.

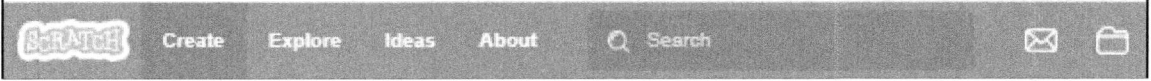

The set of new building blocks that will appear on your screen are shown in the screenshot on the next page. There are various windows, one is to control and set the character of your story another is to set the background of the animations. There are a few buttons on the top of these windows to save, run and stop the project. All the code blocks in different colors are on a long window on the leftmost side. The next window adjacent to the window with all code blocks is the coding window, the work area where we shall be working to create codes. The code blocks can be dragged by the use of mouse click buttons into this working area and can be removed by either dragging back or by using the delete button.

This entire set of code blocks with all windows is known as a scratch platform. We will now discuss major parts of this scratch platform.

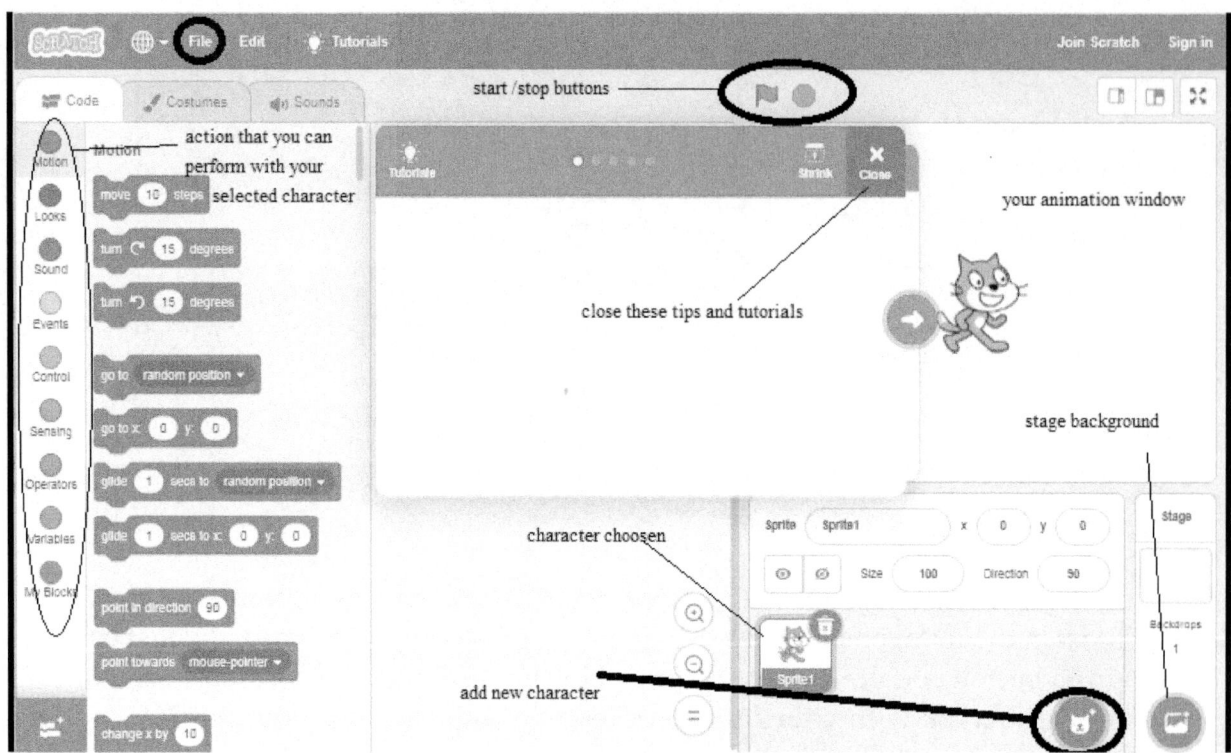

First of all, close the center window that is providing tutorials and tips. The right upper window with the big cat is the animation window. This is the window where the animation created by you will run. The right bottom window with a small cat is the window that shows the characters of the animation, these characters or items of the story or animation used for storytelling are called Sprites in scratch.

The Sprites

Let's say we want to make an animation on a story where only cat and mouse are the two characters. Then this window would contain two characters cat and a mouse. In scratch, we call characters, objects used for drama or storytelling are called "sprites". The characters can always be selected by the plus sign in the sprite window.

Clicking the plus sign in the bottom right of the sprite window to choose or explore new characters provided by the scratch platform.

You will find a lot of animals, people, dance, food, etc in the library. If you put your mouse over images of some of the sprites, especially the images of animals or dance, they will show you some type of repetitive movement.

You can also search any animal, object, or item by its name through the search box provided at the top left corner in the library of the sprite.

You can click anyone to choose

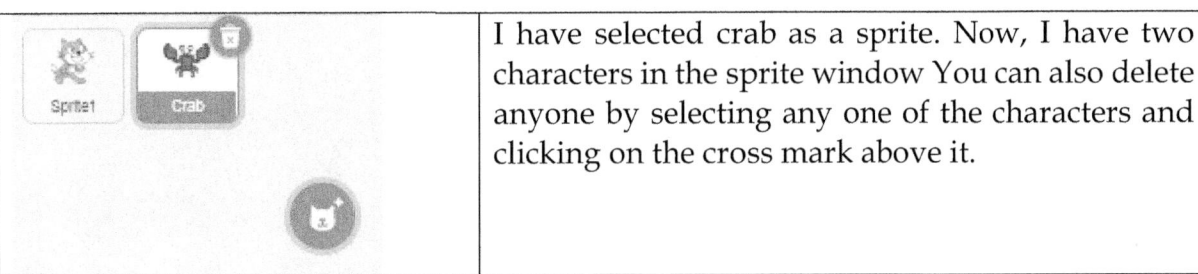

I have selected crab as a sprite. Now, I have two characters in the sprite window You can also delete anyone by selecting any one of the characters and clicking on the cross mark above it.

In some cases, you may not find any suitable sprite, then you can search such images of sprite from google or through any other search engine and upload the same as a new sprite. Uploading a sprite, not available in the library of sprite, may require knowledge of images, their types, and the use of some third-party image editor, therefore for the time being we are not discussing adding custom sprites. We will take up this topic in some other chapters.

The Background

Besides the sprite window, we have a stage window. This is the background before which our characters will move and act at our instructions. New background for the stage can be selected from the plus button at the bottom.

Now, we will explore stage backgrounds available in the system.

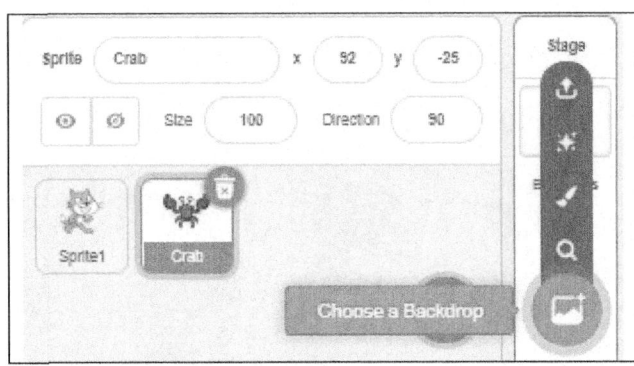

Click on the plus sign below the stage window. Various types of stage backgrounds will appear and you can choose anyone. If your story is about a cat who was a great football player, you can choose football ground as background. If your character is a crab, who was on Malibu beach, select beach background.

The cat with different background will appear on the animation window just above the sprite selection window.

The code blocks

All the code blocks are located on the leftmost window of the scratch platform. These blocks of codes are draggable and can be dragged to the code window or working area for coding purposes.

There are many code blocks and sometimes it becomes difficult to search these blocks of code while making animation for our sprites. Locating appropriate code blocks can be faster, if we try to locate them through various categories like motion, looks, sound, events, controls, sensing, etc.

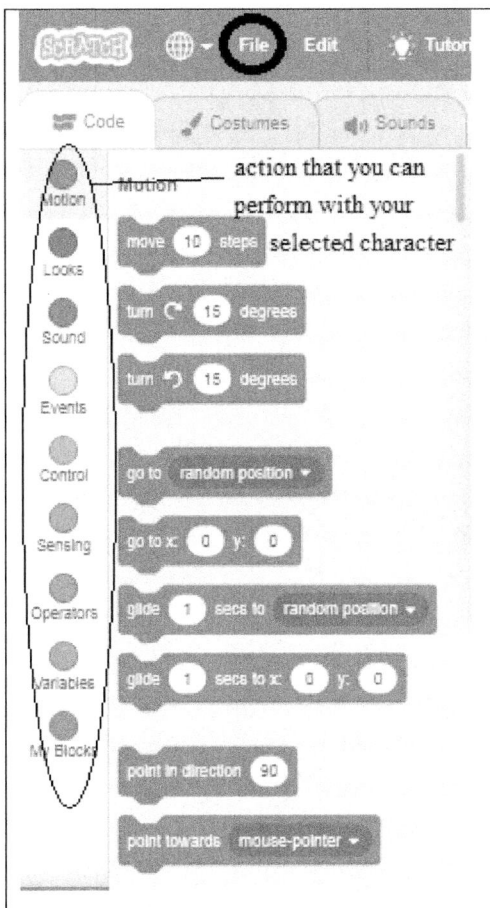

If I want to move my sprite left or right or to make it turn, I will search for the appropriate code block in the motion category. If I am using a mouse click or touch between two different sprites, the appropriate code can be found in the sensing category.

All code blocks have a locking system to get themselves fit with other blocks of code. You will need to attach two or more blocks of codes in the coding area. If you want to remove an individual code of block just put it back or select and press the delete button.

Further, you can execute each block of code before dragging it into the code window by simply double-clicking them.

Let say if, I click move 10 steps and cat sprite is selected. The cat will move some distance towards the right in the animation window.

Scratch allows you to test a code before you use them. You clicked another code "turn 15 degrees" and the sprite selected in the sprite window will rotate a bit. If you feel that this code can serve your purpose, you can drag it into the code window and join it with other codes.

The code window

The code window is the center window which is adjacent to the collection of coding blocks. In the previous section, we have already learned that code blocks from the collection of coding blocks can be dragged in and out of the code window. You can double-click any single code block in the collection of coding blocks to see its functionality.

For each sprite in your animation or story, the code windows are different. Once you select your sprite from the sprite window, the code window for that particular sprite appears in the center and a small image of the sprite can also be located in the top right corner.

	By default, you have a cat as a sprite. If I add carb as another sprite, I can have two sprites in the sprite window. Now, if I select crab in the sprite window, the central code window will allow me to make animation for crab only. The code window for crab will have a small crab image at the top right corner as shown here.

You can now drag code blocks from the collection of code blocks into the code window for crab. I can drag "move 10 steps" three times to the right window of code. Then I can drag the "turn 15-degree" code block and several such codes in the code window. Don't forget to join them. Once you join them in the desired sequence you can run the code for that sprite by just double-clicking the entire sequence of the code block you just created.

You should remember one thing that codes are always executed in a sequence, these are the instructions given to your characters and they are supposed to follow these instructions in the sequence from top to bottom. Once you are complete with the code of crab, you can make code for the cat or any other sprite you have in your animation.

You are the director of the play, you are the owner of the stage and the characters are ready to follow you. Your instruction to move right, turn about, dance, make sound, deliver dialog, all such small instruction given in sequence shall combine to make a perfect animation.

Start/Stop Button

On top of the animation window, we have the start and stop buttons for animation.

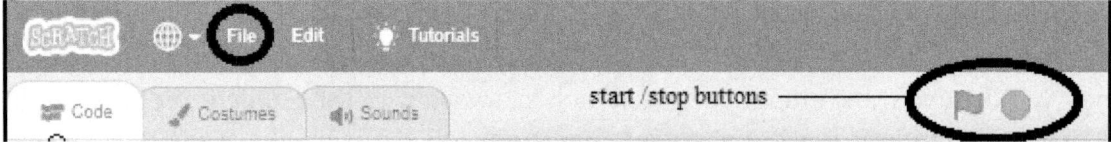

If the code is set in properly, the button with the flag will start the animation and the red round bottom as shown in the screenshot above will stop the animation.

Other parts of the scratch platform

On the left top, we have a file button to save your work.

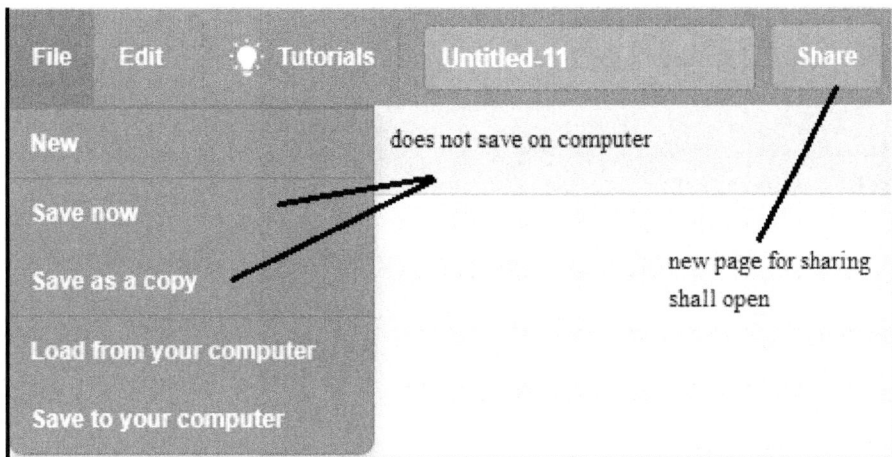

This button can save work done by you either on a computer or can also save it on the scratch platform website. If you want to share your work with your friends or teachers, you should save your work on the website and not on a computer.

Those who are working with software installed on their computer cannot save their work on the website but can only save it on the computer. If they want to share their work with friends or teachers they should log in to the scratch website and upload their work from the computer using the " load from your computer" option as shown above.

The button to share will open a new page for allowing you to share your work. It will provide you the option to write a title, instruction to viewers of your project, it can also allow your friends and teachers to provide comments on the animation you made.

On the right top corner, you have your username displayed, clicking this would allow you to set your profile or to sign out from the system.

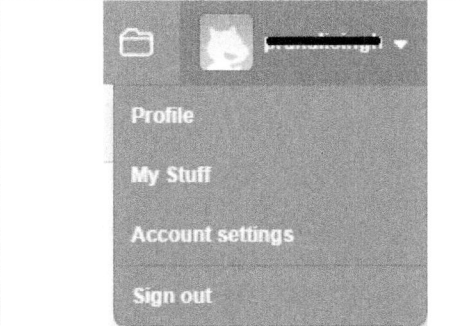	A small folder sign beside your username or the "My stuff" link just below the profile allows you to access all the projects you made and saved on the scratch platform.

We have till now learned to choose characters for our stories and have learned to set stage backgrounds. Now, I know you people are eager to learn animation, the code to move these sprites. In the next chapter, we will make an animation to wish my friend birthday wishes. I want to create a small animation for her and want to wish by my voice-recorded message. Let's see how that can be done.

Assignment

Your homework is to explore all sprites and backgrounds that are available on the scratch platform.

Chapter-2: The Animated Birthday Card

I want to know from you people, what comes to your mind when we say we are going to celebrate a birthday. I have made a list of some items that I want to put in my birthday animation.

1. The cake
2. Balloon
3. Table to put the cake
4. Yourself as a character
5. An indoor background showing a well-decorated house or something like that.

Except for the background, all other items and characters will be known as sprites and for each sprite, we will have a separate coding window and code. If you like you may add more sprites or fewer sprites to your animated card. The above list is just tentative to give us a starting point for the animation.

Setting the stage for animation

Under the stage backdrop window, I found a party background by clicking plus sign that seems to be perfect for the occasion. It has many balloons in the background.

Now, I will search all other items under sprites by clicking plus sign in the sprite window. I found a cake and a character named "Abby". I have selected both of them. I was not able to find any table to put the cake, so I am leaving the table. Balloons are also available in the "party" background, but I still choose one balloon as a sprite. Overall, we have one background and three sprites for this animation.

I have arranged all the sprites i.e. cake, Abby, and balloon on the stage by dragging them and placing them in the right place. The cake was put in the center, the balloon has been arranged with other balloons in the background and Abbey has been set on the left of the cake as if she is looking and watching all the activities. You can do this by just dragging each item by your mouse cursor.

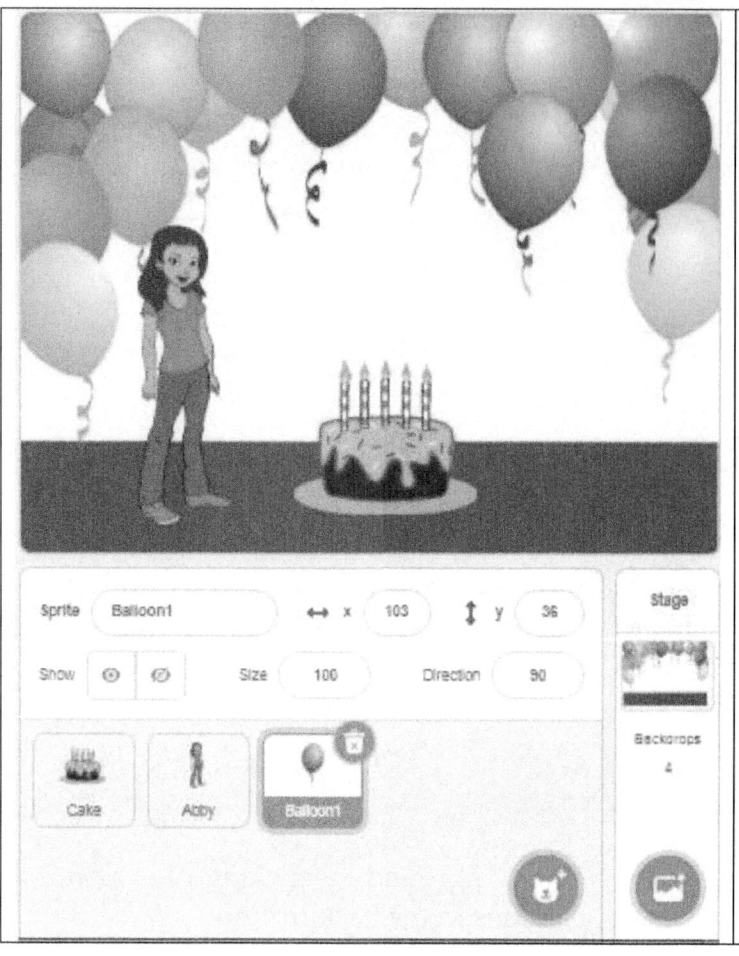

Now, I feel that the stage is set for birthday animation. All that is needed is some type of animation.

Just below the animation window, we have the sprite window. All three sprites are visible here.

We already know that each sprite can be animated separately. I will first start with the balloon. Click and select the sprite balloon in the sprite window. This will open a blank code window for the animation of Balloon in the center of the scratch platform.

The Costumes of Sprites

While selecting each of the sprites you would have noticed that these sprites are capable of showing some type of animation. Abby can make some movements of hands while balloons can change colors and the candles of the cake can light up and go off.

Do you know how such a type of animation can be created? Such animations are created by series of images each having small changes. This is like a flipbook which is a booklet with a series of images, every image gradually changes from one page to the next and when they are viewed in quick succession, the images appear animated.

Here, each sprite that we have selected has many images in sequence, and when they come and go on screen in quick succession, an animated effect is created. The various images of a sprite for animation are known as a costume in scratch.

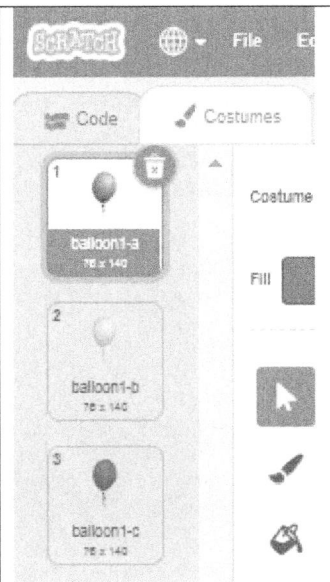	After selecting the balloon from the sprite window, click on the costumes tab which is next to the code tab in right most corner. Here, we can see that it has three color balloons. Costumes allow us to replace the previous image in the animation window with any of the images appearing in the costumes window. The names of the balloons are balloon1-a (blue), balloon1-b (yellow), and balloon1-c (purple). If I replace the blue balloon image with a yellow balloon image. The effect will be a change in the color of the balloon. We can use the costumes to produce such types of effects.
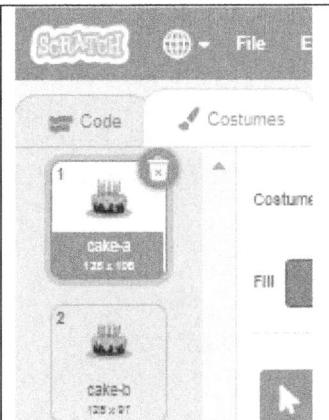	Similarly, the cake has only two costumes, one is with lighted candles and another is a cake with candles gone off. We can also change costumes to create an effect. You can either change them continuously for an effect where candles are going off and are again lighted or can just do it one time to turn off the candles.

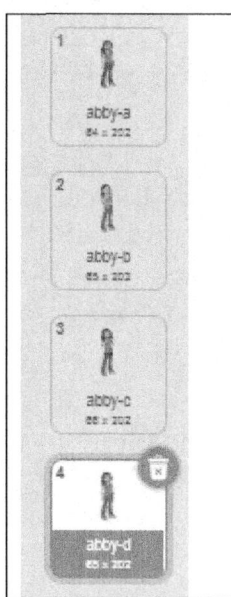

Abby has four costumes, one is standing, another where she is speaking, two another with some hand movements. We can use different images for different occasions to create an effect.

You can choose a reaction of Abby, in the event of a candle been blown off or when a piece of music is played.

Changing Costumes

Now, we will set the action for each sprite individually through the code window. You can access the code window from the "code button" which is at the right top corner of the scratch platform next to costumes.

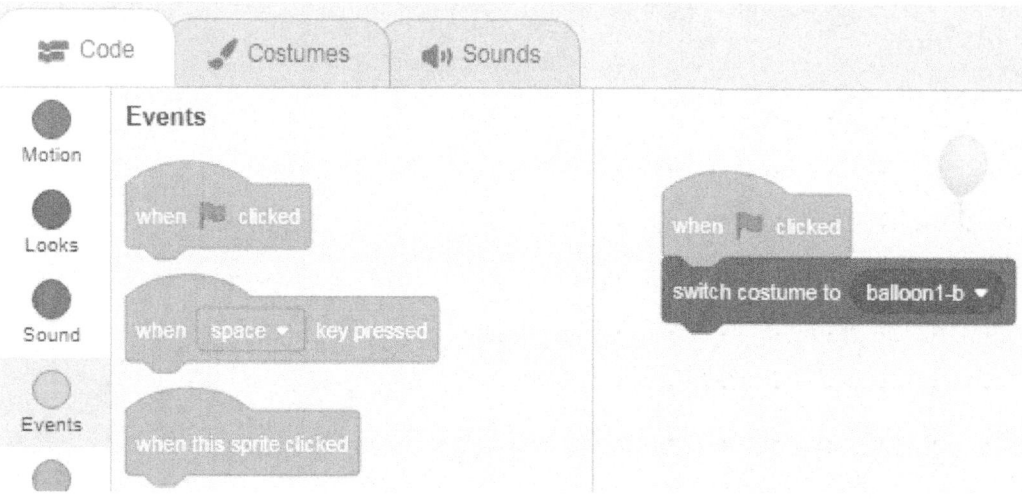

We will first make the balloon to change costume. First, we will select the balloon sprite from the sprite window and then look for a block of the code to change costume. All codes are in the form of blocks on the right-side code window. These code blocks are like building blocks that many of us have used in our childhood for making a house or to construct towers. These blocks of codes can fix within each other. You can drag any code block to the code window of the sprite. The code window of the sprite is the center window where an image of the sprite is appearing in the right top corner. Here in our case, a balloon is appearing in the right corner of the window.

The code blocks are arranged in some categories like motion, looks, sound, events, etc. For a quick search of the code for costume, click on the looks icon appearing on the left side. Look for code that suggests for change of costume. I have found the code block with the name "switch costume to bolloon1-b". I have dragged it into the code window for the balloon.

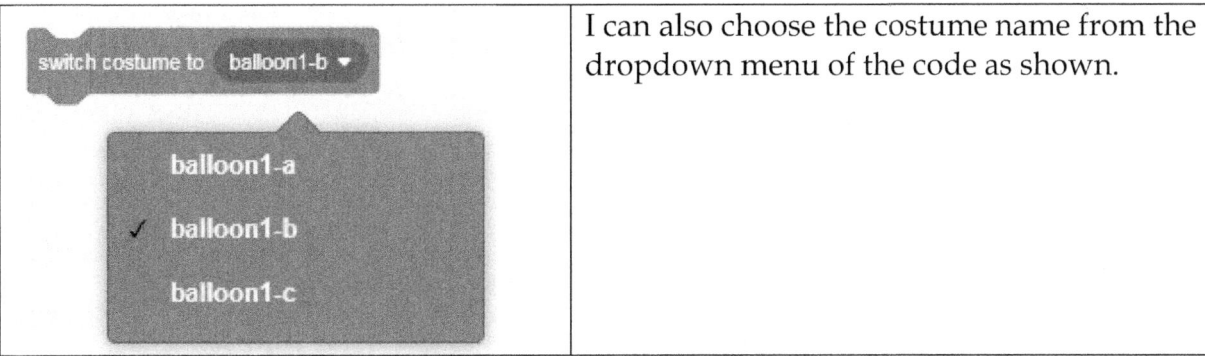

I can also choose the costume name from the dropdown menu of the code as shown.

Another code block that, I want to select is to start the animation for this sprite when I click the start button shown as a flag. This code will be available in the category of events. Click events and look for code block "when the flag is clicked". Drag this code to the code window of the balloon sprite.

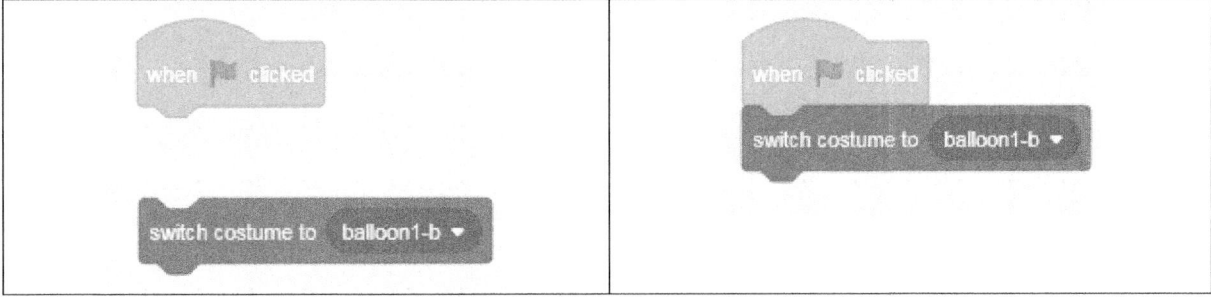

Make sure that the two code blocks join with each other. Now, your code for the balloon to change costume has been created. Click on the flag button at the top of the animation window, the color of the balloon will change to the one selected by you. You can change the balloon1-b costume to balloon-1c and repeat the step. The color will change again.

We have thus completed one step to achieve our objective for changing the color of the balloon. What is missing with this animation?

The color of the balloon is not changing continuously as intended. We need to further modify our code such that the color change is repeated continuously.

The Loops

In computer programming, repeating any task can be achieved by using a loop.

The loops are available under the control icon. Just click the control icon and the major options as they appear are shown below:

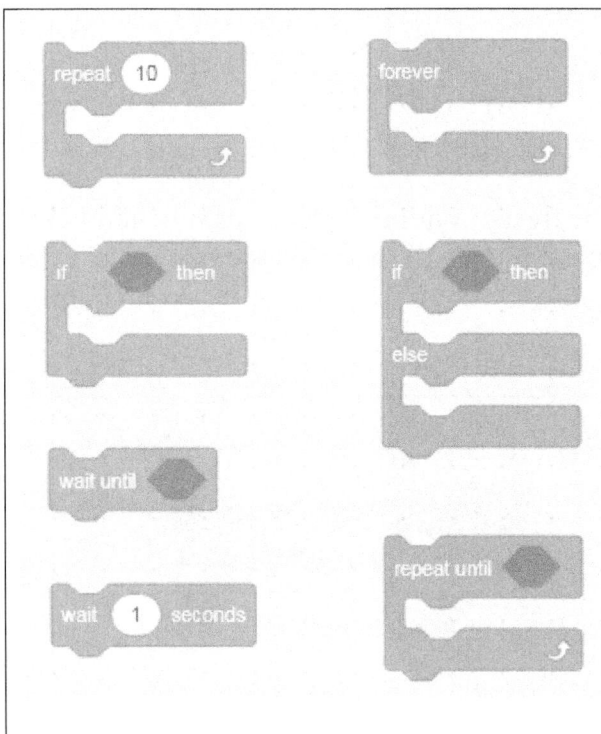

The first one is to repeat 10 times the block that will fit in between. Another code of block is to repeat forever the block of code that fits in between its arms.

Other blocks of codes are conditional block codes which are executed when a certain condition is met. We will come to other blocks of codes in later chapters.

One more code block that is important for us is "wait 1 second". Here, you can change the seconds according to your need. This code of block delays the animation. Suppose, we have a balloon changing code and we repeat it 10 times or forever without putting "wait" block, the color of the balloon will change very fast as if you are watching a movie in fast forward mode.

Now, we will change our balloon sprite code as under :

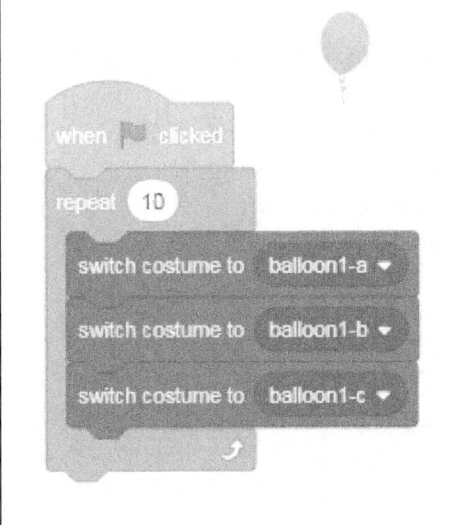	Use your mouse to drag-drop three switch costume codes and arrange them the way, I have shown. When you click start, the three costume change codes will change ten times. Run this code and see the animation. You will notice that nothing has happened or no change was visible. This is because your computer is very fast and can do such types of thousands of repetitions in a second, therefore the change was so fast that your eyes were probably not able to notice the change. We may need to put the wait code in between switch costume blocks.

The Wait code block

Now, try this code with a wait code block in between switch costume block so that the change of costume is not fast and is visible to you. For this purpose, you can select the "wait for 1 second" code block, you may select the control category for locating the code.

The wait 1-second code block allows the user to change the value of seconds from one to any other value. It can also accept values in decimals for example you can put 0.50 seconds for half-second. More is the wait time, slower will be the animation. After each change in the costume, we can add the wait code so that our eyes can observe the change in the color of the balloon. The complete code is presented on the next page.

Always remember, to add a wait code after costume change so that the change can be observed by the user.

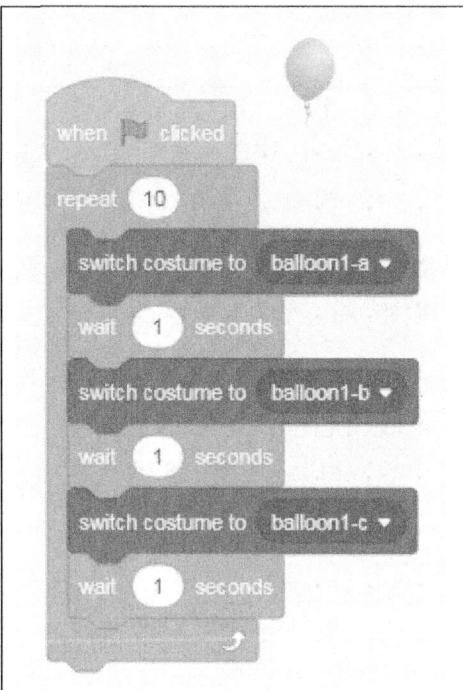

Now when you click the flag button at the top of the animation window, the color of the balloon will change after each second. If you feel the change should be faster, make one second as 0.5 seconds or whatever value smaller than 1 for a faster change of color and greater than 1 for a slower change of color.

Now, can you answer why I have put wait 1-second block after balloon costume block "balloonn1-c"? i.e. just before the end of the loop.

In a loop, the costume is changing from "a" to "b" to "c" and then again to "a". I have put, therefore, put wait block after costume "c" so that there is some delay between again switching to costume "a"

Having done this for the balloon, I will repeat the same with the cake which has two costumes. I will repeat those costumes forever. First, I will select the cake sprite from the sprite window. Now, you will find that the code window has gone blank because we do not have a code for the cake.

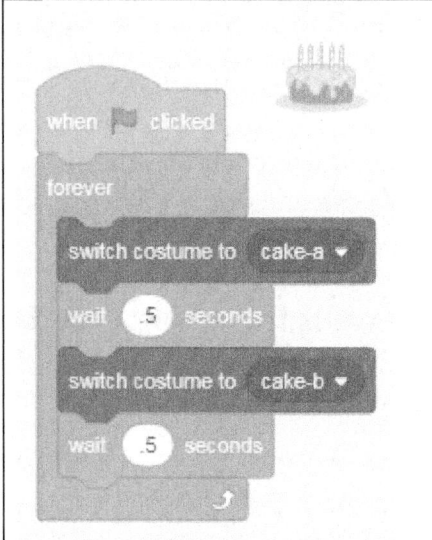

Here, I have put wait seconds as 0.5. The rest of the code is similar to the one that we have used for the balloon. Here, after clicking the flag button, you will find that code for the balloon and cake will run together.

The cake has two costumes only and we have used both of them.

Say and Stop All Code Block

Now we come to the third sprite the girl named "Abby". She has 4 costumes. I have selected few costumes out of the four to have the same good effect.

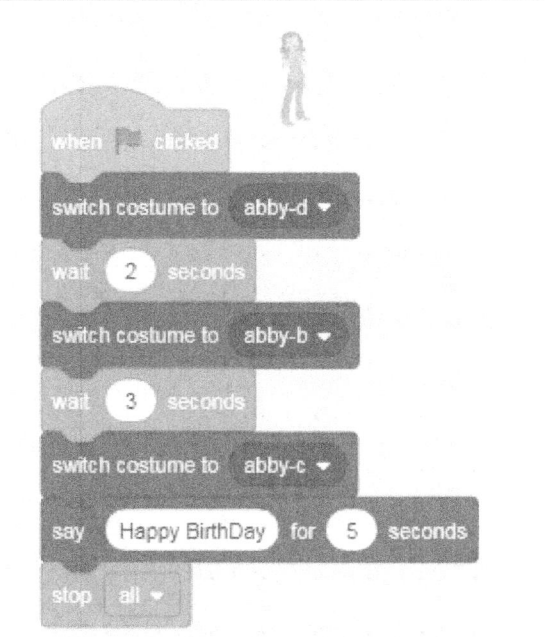

I have chosen three reactions of Abby to be coded as costumes. Here two new blocks of codes have been used.
1. Say
2. Stop All

The "say" block of code can be searched in the "looks" category. This code will create text on the screen as it is shown in comic books. An example is shown below:

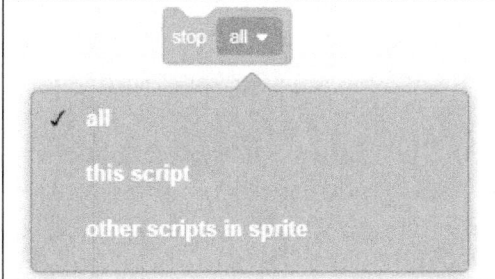

The "stop all" code will stop the animation of this sprite and all other sprites. You can also select to stop animation of this sprite only through the drop-down menu of the stop code block as shown on left.

By use of stop all, the total duration of animation has been decided. Now the animation length will be 10 sec i.e. the length of the Abby script in total. After a total run of 10 seconds, the animation will stop.

Adding Sound/Music to the Animation

I want to deliver a personalized message along with this animation. Then I also have an option to record my voice and play along with the animation. You can also download some "happy birthday music" and add the same to the animation.

It is simple, you have to just select the "play music" block of code. The code block is available under the sound category.

You can add this code of block to any of the sprites as a separate block. Leaving the one that we created earlier for change of costume intact.

You can record any personalized message by clicking the dropdown menu of the play sound and clicking the record button. Give it a name, I have given the name happy Birth Day.

Make sure that the length of the recorded message is not more than the animation length that we have created i.e. 10 seconds.

Now, I just want to ask, why I have created a separate block of code and not included the same with the Abby costume change block. The answer is till the sound will be played, Abby will stop animating. You can try adding the sound to Abby's code and notice the changes that appear.

With this, I hope that you are ready to send anyone a personalized greeting on birthday or Xmas or new year or whatever is the occasion.

Now, you can save your project by clicking the file at the top corner of the window. Make a habit of saving the file once you have made some changes. Here, below are some images of the animation that we have created. Of course, you can have a feel of the type of animation that has been created but you will not be able to hear my personalized message through images.

One of the balloons is also changing color, however, in case you are reading the black and white paperback version of this book, you won't be able to locate the balloon.

Can you add your image as a sprite? Yes, you can! All you have to do is to take your photograph and cut the surroundings in an image editor tool neatly. You can use Adobe Photoshop for this purpose. Also, you have to make sure that the background of the image is transparent. We will again touch on this topic of transparent images in upcoming chapters.

Assignment

Try to add one pet on the other side of the cake.

Chapter 3: Practice loop and movements

The MSWlogo is an old programming language that was being used for creating the computerized logo, designs, and also for learning basic concepts of computer programming. At scratch, we can do all the stuff that an MSWlogo can perform. In this chapter, we will learn to draw basic shapes like squares, rectangles, circles, etc. We will be using many of the code blocks that we had just used in our last script.

Drawing of basic shape will be fun and will also develop your programming skills.

Exploring pen extension

The scratch has many extensions available for doing some advanced work like linking your computer to hardware for programming a moveable car, reading light sensors, touch sensors, temperature sensors it can be used for making robots that can move.

Some of these extensions will also be used in our book. In this section, we will be using an extension "pen". This extension will provide us pen and with the help of that pen, we can program the pen to draw simple shapes like squares, rectangles, and circles. When we gain some experience with these programming skills and pen, we will try to draw complex drawings.

To add a pen tool and its related command blocks to your tool kit, you have to add the extension on the scratch platform. Look at the left corner of the scratch platform, you will find the icon as shown below:

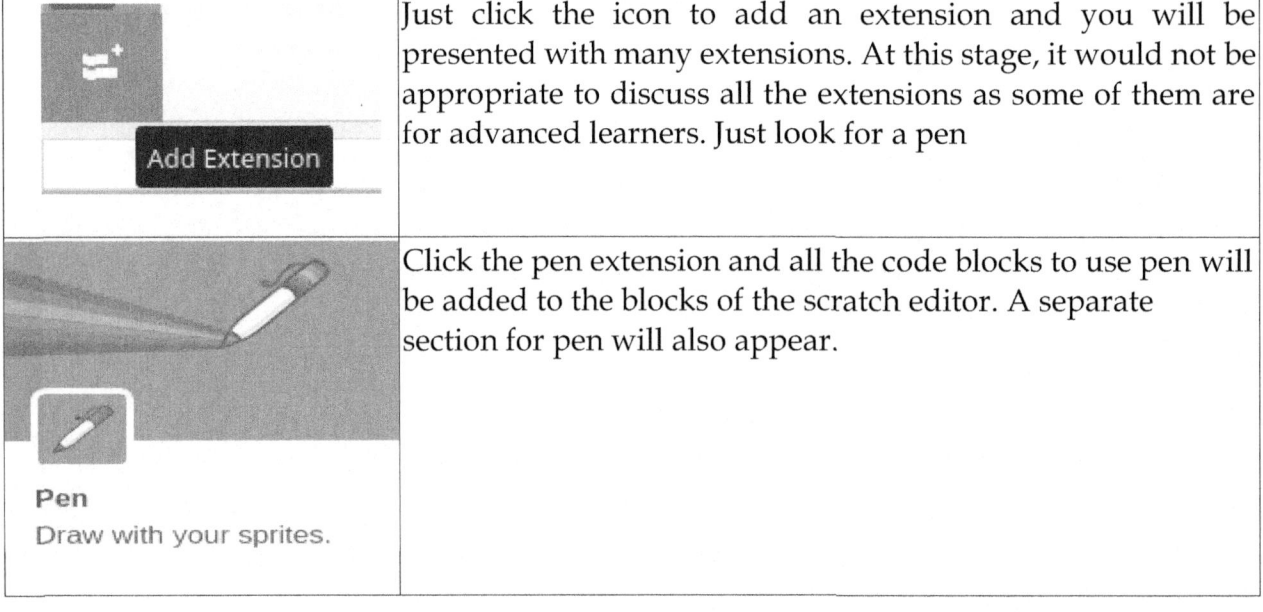

	Just click the icon to add an extension and you will be presented with many extensions. At this stage, it would not be appropriate to discuss all the extensions as some of them are for advanced learners. Just look for a pen
	Click the pen extension and all the code blocks to use pen will be added to the blocks of the scratch editor. A separate section for pen will also appear.

Now, let's explore some of the code blocks, before we use them one by one.

pen down / pen up	As the name suggests, pen down will allow you to write on the screen and pen up will not allow you to write on the screen. Say you want to write "i" on the screen with a dot. To mark the dot you would be required to pen up and then pen down at the appropriate location.
set pen color to	This will allow you to set the color of your pen ink. You can choose the color of your choice by clicking on the color-picking option.
change pen size by (1) / set pen size to (1)	These two options are to increase the size of a pen. If you increase the size the line drawn will be bold.
change pen color by 10 / set pen color to 50	Here, in place of color, you can also choose brightness, saturation, transparency. Now, if you want to know what does color 10 or color 70 mean? Then probably, you have to explore the "set pen color" option discussed above.
erase all	As the name suggests, this block of code when activated will clear the entire screen.
stamp	The image of the sprite will get printed on the screen. We will come to it in detail in upcoming sections.

Drawing using Pen

When you instruct the computer to pen-down, it is an instruction to the computer to put a pen on the screen for drawing purposes. If you ask your computer to pen up, the computer will keep removing the pen from the screen so that it cannot make the drawing.

Now we will attempt to draw a line on the screen. The code is shown below:

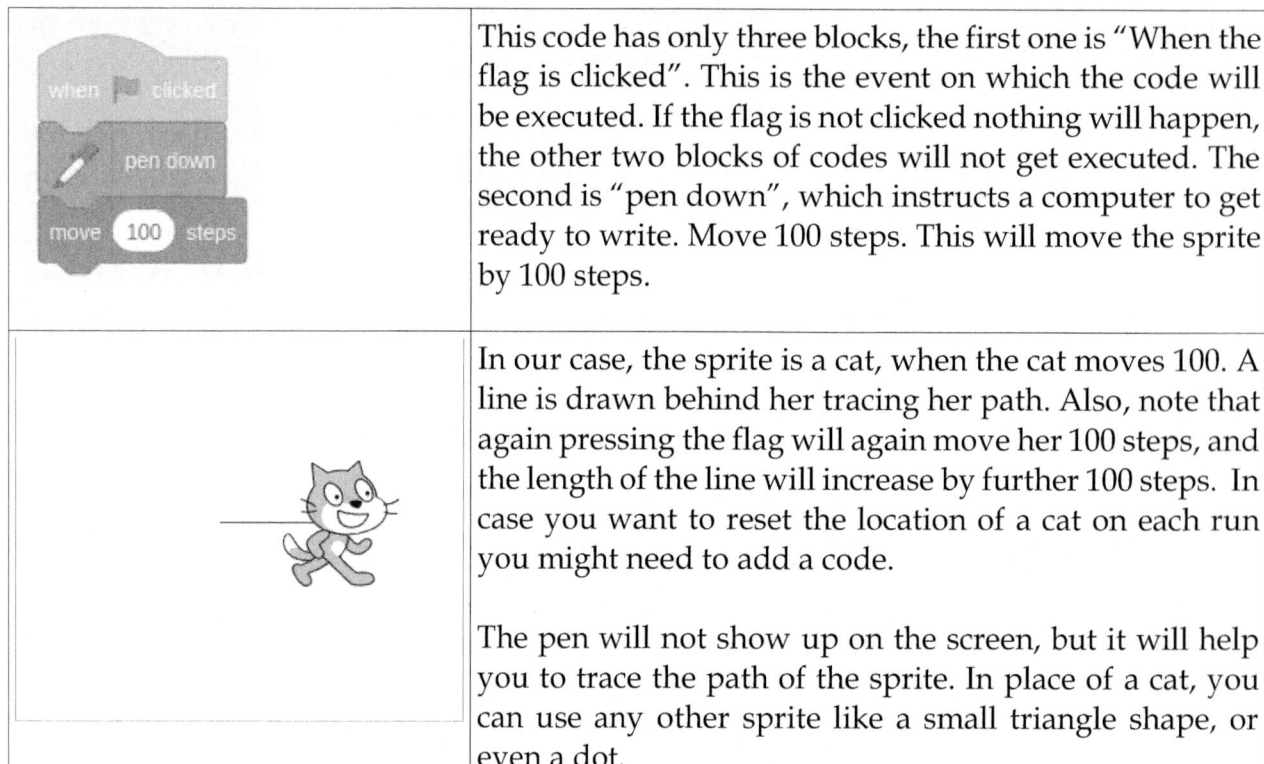

(code blocks: when flag clicked, pen down, move 100 steps)	This code has only three blocks, the first one is "When the flag is clicked". This is the event on which the code will be executed. If the flag is not clicked nothing will happen, the other two blocks of codes will not get executed. The second is "pen down", which instructs a computer to get ready to write. Move 100 steps. This will move the sprite by 100 steps.
(cat sprite with line drawn behind)	In our case, the sprite is a cat, when the cat moves 100. A line is drawn behind her tracing her path. Also, note that again pressing the flag will again move her 100 steps, and the length of the line will increase by further 100 steps. In case you want to reset the location of a cat on each run you might need to add a code. The pen will not show up on the screen, but it will help you to trace the path of the sprite. In place of a cat, you can use any other sprite like a small triangle shape, or even a dot.

Re-set sprite after each run

Sprites are characters of your animation or play or story. If a story starts from a palace and ends in a forest then if you try to re-run the script, the script will start from the forest. If in an animation a car has to move from left to right and someone stops the code in-between and when the code is re-run the car will start moving from the point it was stopped previously. You have already seen it in our earlier example. Each time you press the flag button, the cat sprite will move 100 steps from the location where she left.

As a good programmer, everyone should initialize their stage, sprites, and other components of code to initial values before animation or script starts.

Here, in this case, I have added the following codes for initialization of sprite and screen before code can be run.

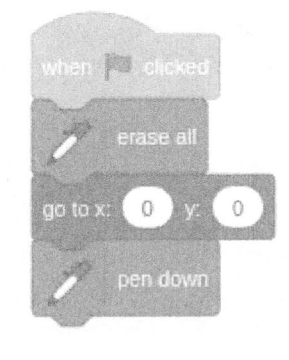	When working with a pen, we need a clear screen before the start of the script each time. To clear the screen from any drawing we can use the "erase all" block of code. Another requirement is we reset our sprite, say I want to keep my sprite at the center then we can instruct the computer to go to x=0 and y=0. In case, you want to keep your sprite at some other place on the extreme left corner, you can use x=-200 and y=-200. More about this x,y values as been discussed below for better understanding. We don't know at what point the script is stopped by the user. In every run, we need to ensure pen position whether it is pen down or pen up. I set it to pen down at the starting of the script.

Let's first understand how locations are defined in scratch animations. The screen may be assumed to be divided into grids, the center of the screen is denoted as x=0 and y=0. If you want to move high then you have to increase y and if you want to move down you have to give a value of y in minus.

Similarly, if you want to move to the right value of x will increase from zero and if you want to move to the left from the center, the value of x will be negative.

The range of x will be about -200 to 200, where -200 means extreme left and +200 means extreme right location on the screen. Similarly, the range of y will also be about -200 to +200, where -200 means extreme bottom and +200 means extreme top.

A graphical representation of the screen grid is provided here.

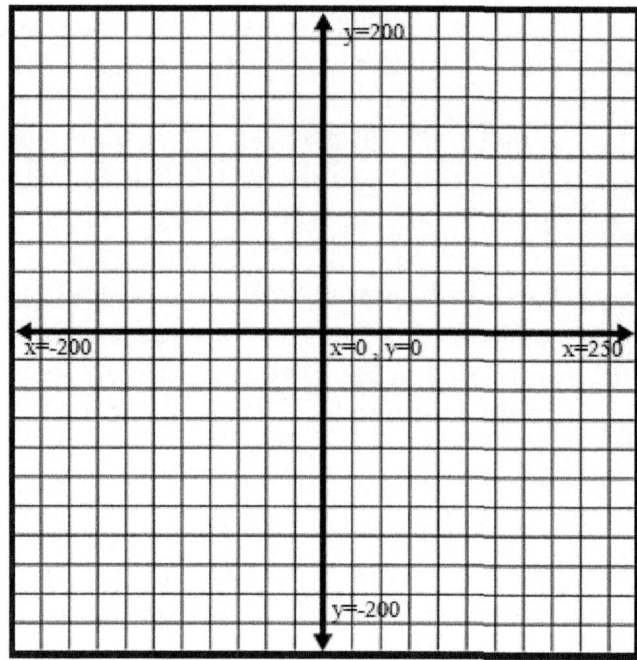

Any location in the right upper square will have positive x and positive y values.
Any location in the left upper square will have negative x and positive y values.
Any location in the left bottom square will have negative x and y values
Any location in the right bottom square will have positive x and negative y values.

Having understood the range and the way, locations are represented on screen we can move any of our sprites to a particular location.

Drawing a square on the screen

Before you make a square on the screen using scratch, I suggest you draw a square on paper without lifting the pen. I assume that you will follow the below path for making a square.

For making a square, you have to draw a straight line, you will turn 90 degrees in an anti-clock direction and again draw a straight line of the same length. You will again have to take a 90-degree turn in the anti-clock direction and draw another equal length line and the last line will be drawn after taking a 90-degree anti-clockwise turn and your square is ready.

I have also followed the same for drawing a square from scratch. The full code to draw a square is given below for your understanding.

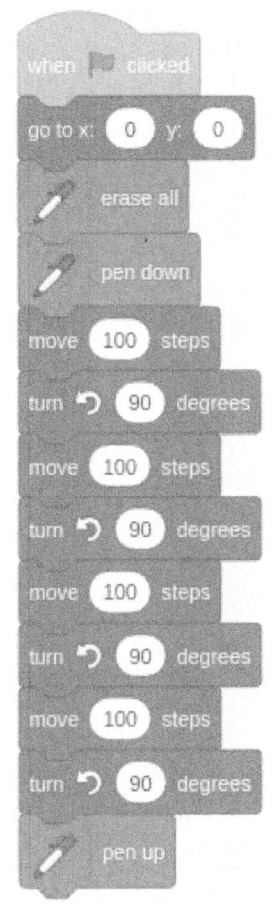

The first 4 blocks are to initialize our screen, location, and pen. While my pen is down, i.e. the pen is in writing mode, I have moved 100 steps. This will trace the path of my sprite and a straight line with length 100 will be drawn on the screen. Now, I have made a 90-degree turn in the anti-clock direction. The anti-clock direction is shown on the block where it is written "turn 90 degrees".

The same code has been repeated three more times to draw the other three lines of the square.

Lastly, I have a pen up. So that no further drawing is drawn on the screen.

In case, you are not familiar with the degrees, I suggest you ask your mathematics teacher or parents to explain them to you. In the chapter for the pong game, I have a small section to help you with directions. I hope, it can help you with some concepts regarding directions.

Drawing square with a loop

Now we will use loop code to make a square.

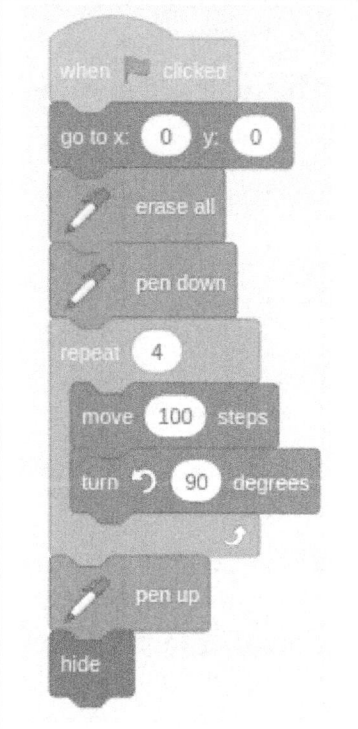

On the left is the code for drawing the square, I have improved the code. I have used repeat code to reduce the size of the code. In the last code, we had used to move 100 steps and turn 90-degree anti-clock 4 times. In place of repeating the code itself, I can use a repeat loop. I have set a repeat loop to repeat the code four times and included "move 100 steps" and "turn 90-degree" code blocks between its two arms as shown on the left side.

This will also create the square. Here, I have also used code block hide at the end of the code. This hide code block can be found in the "looks" set of blocks. This will hide the sprite cat and we will only have a square on the screen without a cat.

Drawing pattern from a square

In this section, we will be making a pattern using squares.

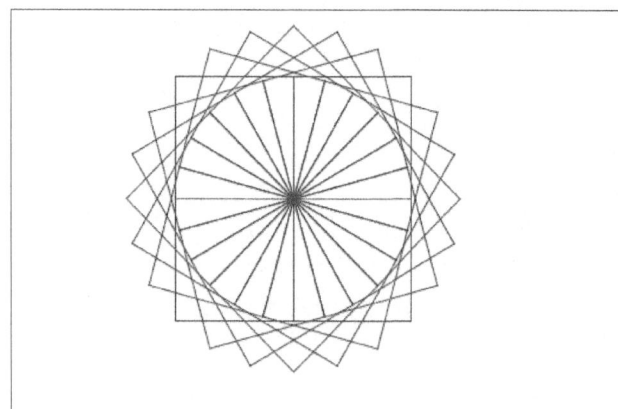

We will draw many squares. Each square will start from the same point however, each one will be slightly rotated from the previous one. Drawing of all these squares on the screen will make the design shown on the left side.

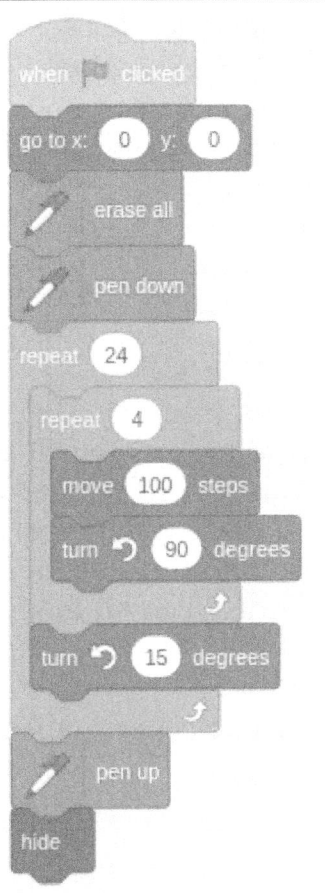

The only code block that I have added to the last scratch script is a loop to make 24 squares and to turn each square by 15 degrees anti-clock direction.

Why I have to make 24 squares? The answer to this question is that a full round is 360 degrees. If I rotate by 15 degrees each time, I will need to move 24 times to complete a circle. 24 X 15 = 360. If you make a loop lesser than 24 with each turn of 15 degrees, the pattern will look incomplete.

You can choose a 10-degree rotation each time, in this case, you will need to make 36 squares and if you make a 12 degree turn each time, you will need to make 360 divided by 12 = 30 squares to complete your pattern.

In the code on the left, after the formation of each square, you need to make a 15-degree turn. So the code block to turn 15 degrees is put after completion of the repeat 4 times block used for making square in the last example.

The entire procedure for making square is since required to be performed 24 times another repeat block has been added wherein inside its arms, we have put square making blocks and to turn them by 15 degrees after each square is completed. You can also add a code block to change color by 10 along with a turn 15-degree code block to have a colorful pattern. The Hardcopy of this book is since going to be without colors, I am not including this in the example.

Drawing letter "A" on screen

In this section, we will attempt to draw the "A" alphabet on screen. Below, we draw The alphabet, I encourage you to write A on paper with a pen. The condition is that you will not make "A" without lifting your pen.

I am representing my method of writing "A" without lifting my pen to draw the diagram.

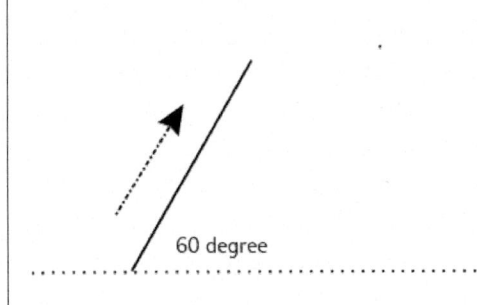	If the sprite is facing to the right of this book, first I will have to turn my pen by 60-degree anti-clock direction and draw a straight line. This line will be 60 degrees from the base. If you feel that the slope of a line is more or less, you can choose any other angle, but you may need to adjust other angles according to your choice.
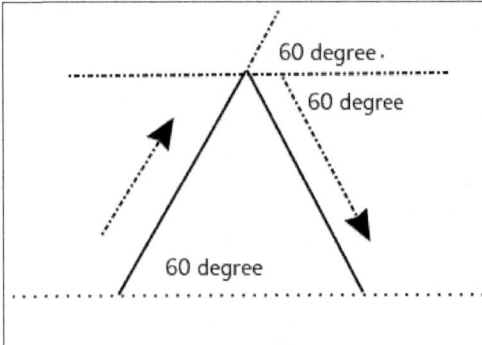	Now, my pen direction is facing inclined 60 degrees upward. I need to move clockwise 60 degrees to align my pen directly to the right side of this book. I will need a further 60 degrees for setting the direction of the pen inclined downward. When all is set, I can draw the line. In total, we need a 120-degree clock-wise turn before the line can be drawn.
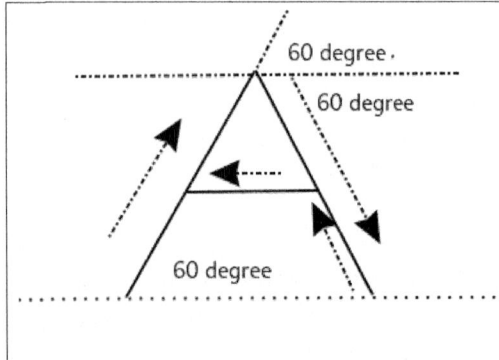	Now the last step is to draw a horizontal line without lifting the pen. I can trace back half the path I covered. A move of 60-degree counter-clock direction will make my pen face the right side of the book again. Now I can move backward i.e. in the negative direction to complete the letter "A"

All the steps discussed above have been used in the script for drawing the "A" alphabet.

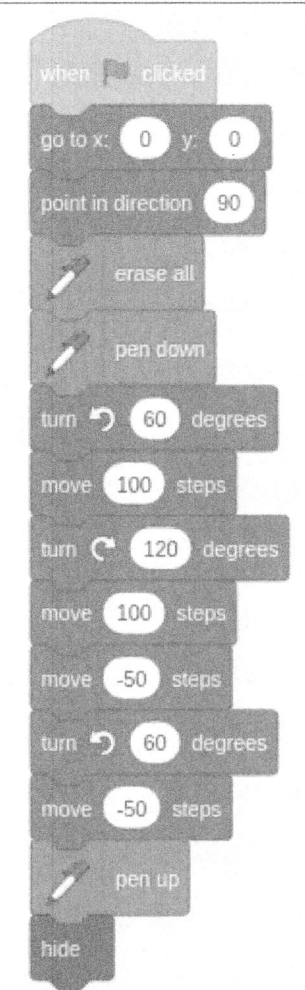

The first five blocks on the left are for initialization of sprite location, pen, and screen. Here, an additional code "point in direction 90" has been used to set the initial direction of the sprite. After initialization, the default cat sprite will face the right side of the book.

I will follow all the steps provided in the above diagrams. First, turn 60 degrees counter clock-wise and move 100 steps to draw the first line.

Turn 120-degree clockwise direction and move 100 steps to draw the second line.

Move -50 steps i.e. trace back the initial path by moving backward.

Turn 60 degrees counter clock direction so that our direction is again facing the right side of the book. Now more -50 steps i.e. move backward to complete formation of alphabet "A".

The last step is to hide the sprite and pen up.

Star Pattern

The code and result are shown below for you. Each angle is 144 degrees and the lines are 200 steps.

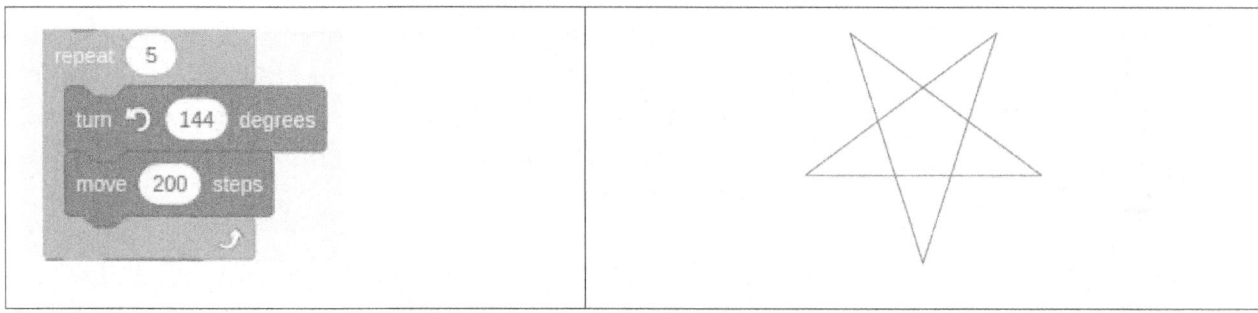

To save the number of pages in the book. I am not repeating the initialization part. You can add yourself.

Drawing Circle

There is no block to draw a circle. We can work around and draw a circle by the code given below.

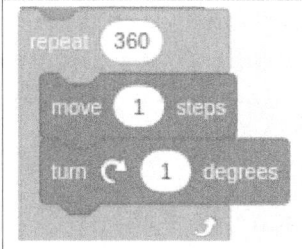

By this time we already know that a full round has 360 degrees. If we move one step and move 1 degree we will be able to make a circle.

The circle thus drawn will have a boundary with a length of 360 steps. This 360 is the perimeter of the circle. The radius of the circle can be calculated using the formula of the circle. i.e. perimeter divided by 2 pis. There the circle that we can draw from the code will have a radius of 57.32 steps.

Pattern created from a Circle

This pattern will take time to get drawn. You can sit back and observe while the computer creates it for you. You can create many other patterns or create your pattern using scratch. You can search for MSWlogo patterns on google and try to re-create them using scratch.

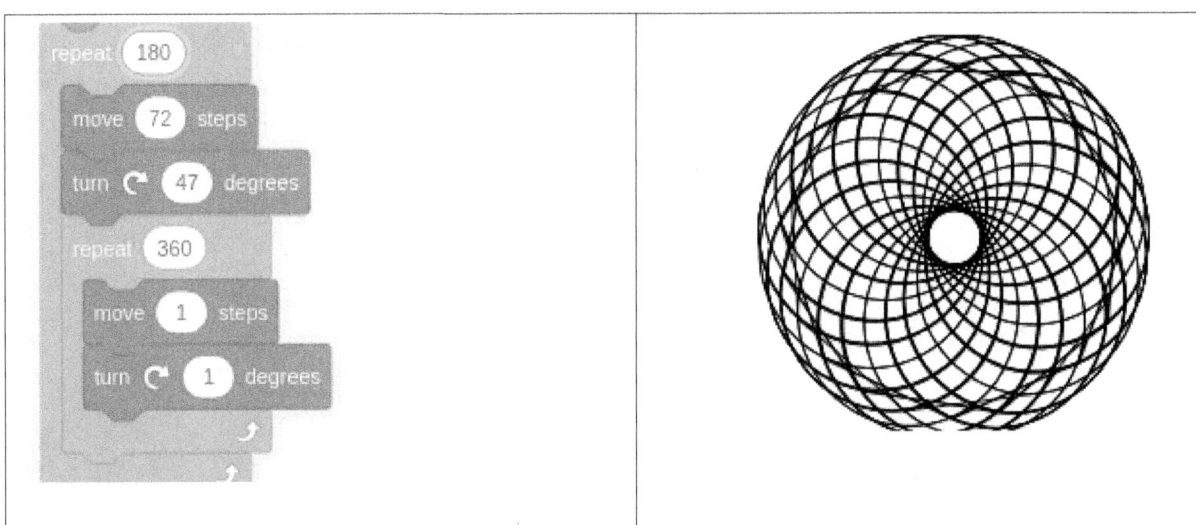

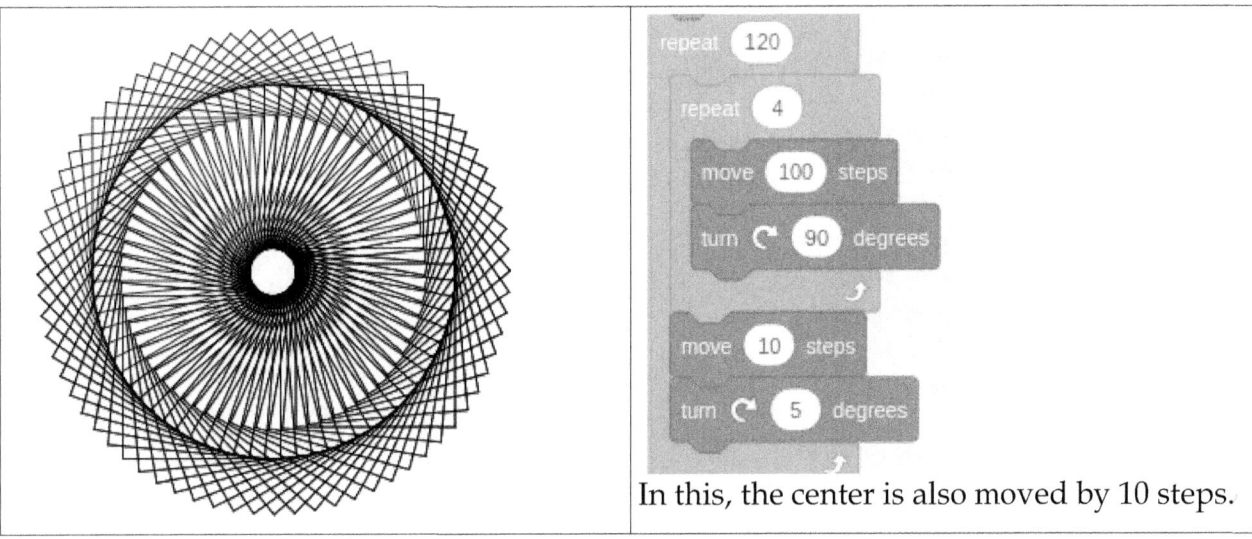

In this, the center is also moved by 10 steps.

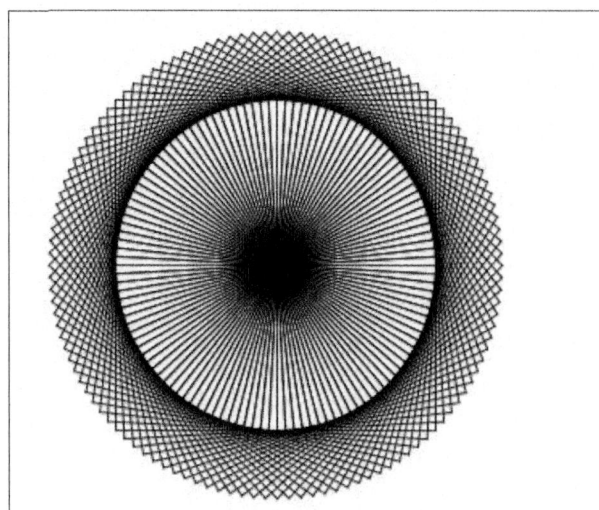

Rotate square by 3 degrees 120 times.

Note angle is a prime number and 3 X 120 is 360 degree.

You can make your patterns with any shape.

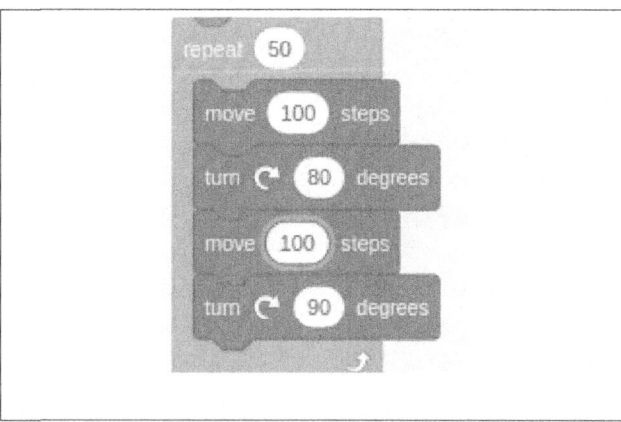

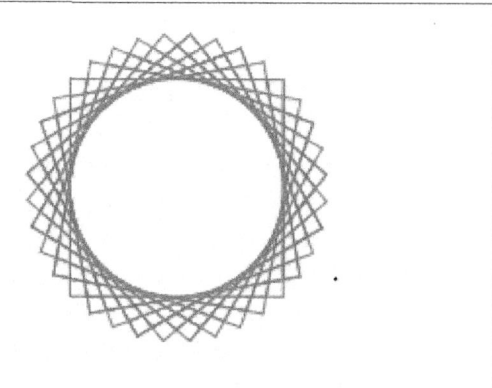

Trick: keep angle a prime number and try repeating various patterns such that angle X repetition = 360. Also, change color to have better designs.

Assignment

1. Draw Triangle with each side 100 steps and each angle as 60 degrees (please note the sum of all angles of a triangle is always 180 degree)

2. Draw a staircase with 10 steps. Each step will have a height of 20 steps and a length of 20 steps.

3. Draw a pattern with side length 110, angle 47, and circle. Repeat them 180 times.

Chapter 4: Giving motion to Sprites

Animation is all about moving your spirits. We have already used some functions in the previous chapters for the movement of sprites for drawing patterns. At scratch, you have the option to move your sprites. The three most popular mode of motions are as under :

Goto Random Position

Random means that do not have any sequence. This type of motion makes the sprite disappear and reappear at any location on the screen. In such a type of motion, you will not be able to know the location of the sprite where it will reappear. This type of motion cannot be controlled and is normally used in games to generate points or game hurdles at any place to make the game challenging each time you place. This can also be used if you do not want to control the motion of that sprite. An example is the last project wherein we had created birthday wishes through animation. Here we can move the balloon from one location to another location. The modified code for this is given below:

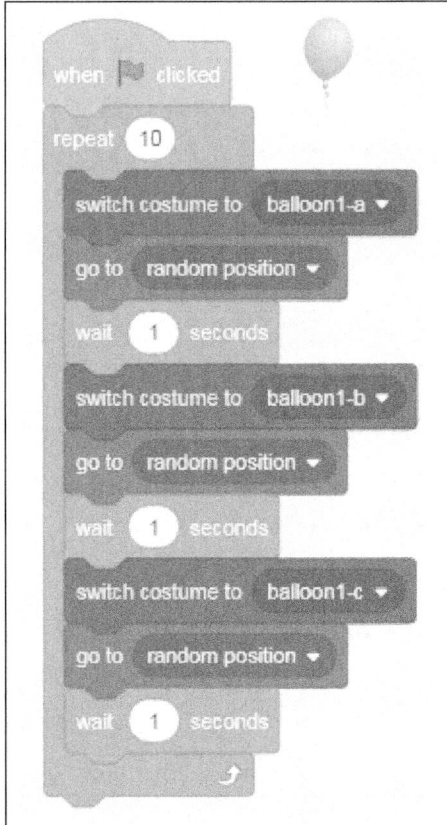

In this code for sprite for the balloon. I have added the "goto random position" code block after a costume change. This will make the sprite disappear and reappear at some other location of its own choice with a changed costume.

Make the change to your animation made in the last project and observe the changes. You will feel as if the balloon is moving. I have added this code block at three places after each costume change. You can make it happen once or twice per loop.

I hope with this example, it is clear how a goto random code block will work. If you add random to the cake, the cake will start disappearing and reappearing anywhere on the screen.

Glide

As the name suggests glide allows movement of sprite from one location to another location without disappearing and reappearing. This can be done in many ways. For the time being, I have changed the code of the balloon sprite of the last project to show how it works.

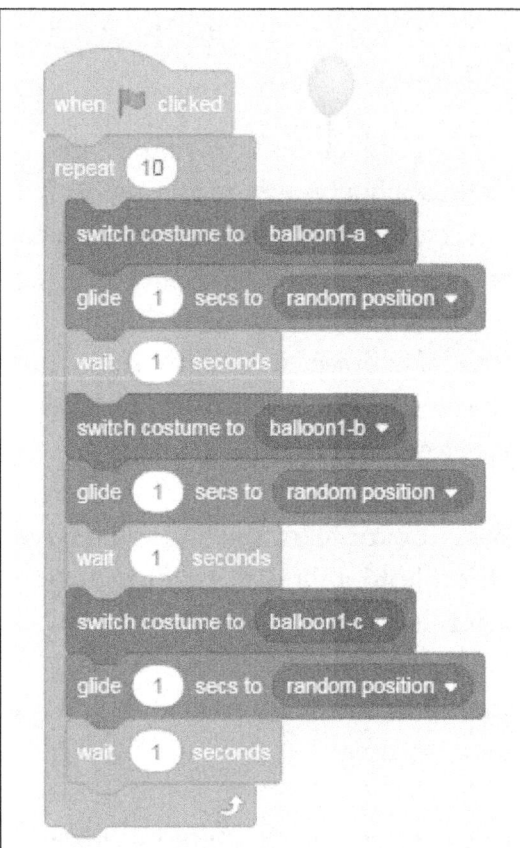

I have replaced the last "goto random position" code with "glide 1 secs to random position".

This random position will again allow the system to choose the next position of the balloon on its own, however, the "glide 1 second" will allow the balloon to move in one sec from one location to another location without disappearing. You may modify your code for the last project by selecting the glide option from the motion category of code.

You will find that this type of animation gives better results than the birthday wishing animation.

Move to x and y

The third way is a controlled way for moving your sprite. You have some prior experience of working with graphs then this would be an added advantage. We have already discussed moving to the x and y code block in the previous chapter when we moved our sprite to the center of the screen by using values x=0 and y=0.

I have an example of a dancing girl over here to explain what we have learned so far.

Dancing Girl project

Select a suitable background for the stage suitable for a dancing girl as shown below:

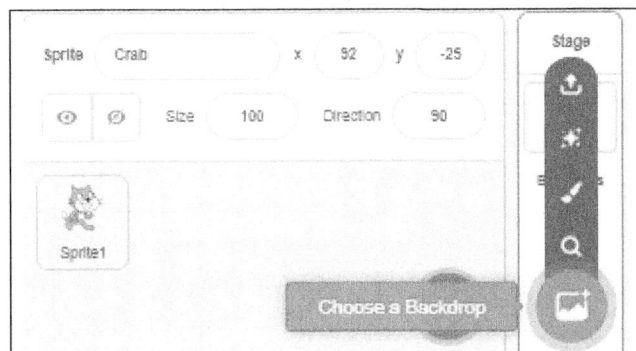

Click on the plus sign below the stage window. Various types of stage backgrounds will appear and you can choose anyone. Here for the dancing girl, I have selected "Theater" background

Similarly, we will select the sprite "ballerina" by clicking plus sign in the sprite window. I have selected, ballerina as the sprite has many costumes and since you already know how to use costume change code block, you will be able to take full advantage of the sprite.

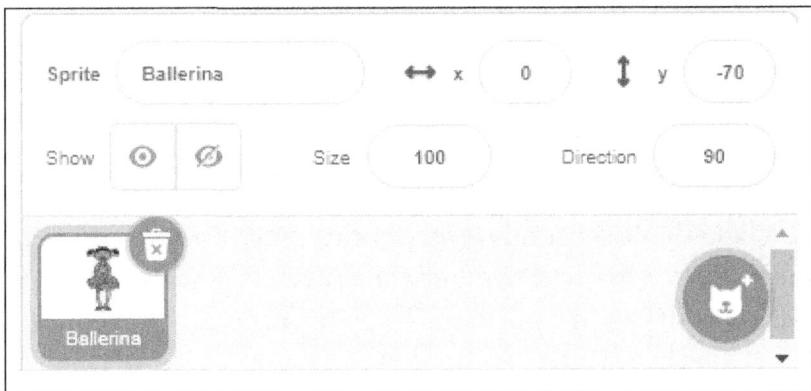

I have dragged the sprite in the center location of the background and on the floor of the theater background. In the window of sprite, you can notice that the location of x and y are automatically appearing. In my case, it is x=0 and y=-70.

Further, if you feel that the size of a sprite is too small or too large as compared to the background the same can also be changed from here by changing the value of size. Reducing the value from 100 will reduce the size of the sprite and increasing the value of size above 100 will increase the size of the sprite.

You already know how to change the costume, you can use the code for change of costume to generate dance and can also use an appropriate value of wait code to adjust the speed of the dance. I want ballerina, the sprite to cover the entire stage by her movement on the left and right sides.

I have made ballerina dance in the center and have glide to the right side of the stage, dance and then glide her to the left side of the stage and finally end the dance by bringing her to the center. In the code, I have used the "next costume" code instead of the "switch costume code" block. We are since using all the costumes to generate dance effects, next costume will help improve the readability of the code and reduce the size of the code block.

On the next page is the entire code written for the "ballerina" sprite. The first block of code is "when the flag is clicked". It is usually every code's first block in scratch. The second code is to goto x = 0 and y=-70. This part we have already seen while setting the stage for the ballerina. This position is the center position of sprite and onto the ground of theater.

Now, you may ask me a question, why I have put this code line over here when we had manually set the stage by dragging the ballerina onto its right location. This has been done because, after many runs, ballerina may end her dance at a different location than the place from where she started. In such cases, this code ensures that before the code and dance re-starts on the next execution, she is at the right place.

Similarly, we have another set of codes that set the costume of the ballerina as the first costume. This is again done to ensure that before the code and dance start, the ballerina is in the right dance position or right costume.

All the code blocks which are written to ensure that the sprites and backgrounds are at the right place and right location before execution of script are known as code for initialization. Here, by the code goto x and y positions and switch costume to the first costume, we are initializing the program code so that before the execution everything is set to initial position. If someone presses the stop button while dace is under execution, the ballerina will get stop at a random place in a random costume and if we again press the flag button, the ballerina reset herself to the center of the stage with the right costume.

To know the difference, you can execute the above code with and without initialization code blocks as discussed above and notice the difference. The rest of the code is straightforward, I have used glide code block three times in this code. This glide code will help ballerina to move to the right side of the stage after performing in the center of the stage, she can then perform on the right side of the stage and then can again move to the left of the stage and then to the center.

You can again ask me the question, why I have not used the goto code block and why I have chosen the glide code block? The answer to this question is that the goto code block will make ballerina disappear from the initial location and make her appear at other places, The effect will be ghostly i.e disappearing and reappearance. You can try also try the goto code block in place of the glide code block and try to observe the difference in the movement of the ballerina.

Chapter 5: Pong Game (Ball Bouncing)

Ping Pong game is a game in which the ball bounces off the edges and when it is about to fall you have a movable paddle, you support the ball from the bottom with a movable paddle and if you fail to bounce the ball, the game gets over.

Before we make this game of bouncing ball, we need to know the sprites required. The answer is a paddle and a ball. Select a cool background.

Bouncing Ball from edge

You need to create the entire code for bounce, we already have a code of "if on edge, bounce" under the motion category of codes. This code bounces sprite when they reach the end of the screen. A simple code to bounce a ball is given below. Before you use the code, choose a ball or balloon as a sprite and a cool background for the stage.

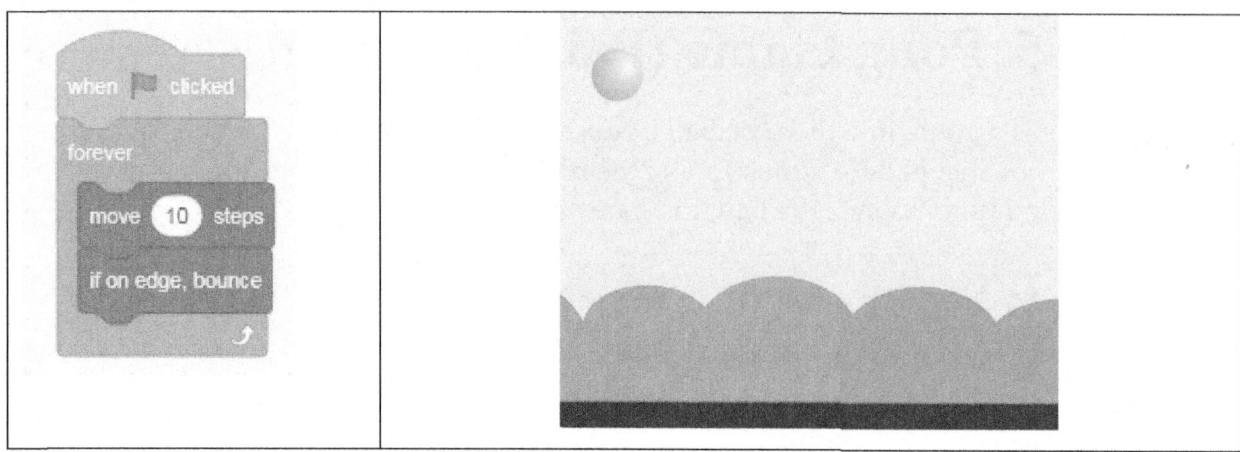

As soon as the code is executed for ball sprite, the code goes in for a forever loop. The first code of line is to move 10 steps. This command increases or decreases the value of x and y together depending on the direction of the sprite. We have still not covered the direction topic, we will come to it later on. For a while, you can assume that this helps a movement of 10 steps in the direction of the sprite.

The second code is "if on edge, bounce". This is a magic code that automatically detects that the ball has reached the other end of the screen and it needs a bounce. Just a few code blocks can create the ever-bouncing ball on the screen. You can add the above code block to the ball sprite and run to see the effect.

The second sprite that is required is a paddle for making the ball bounce from the bottom. could not found any suitable sprite that can act as a paddle. There is a "line" named sprite, I selected the "line" as the sprite. The size of the line sprite was too long for our purpose. One option is that I change the size of the sprite to a smaller value than 100. The size of the sprite can be changed from the sprite window after selecting the sprite. The second option is to reduce the size by editing the line in the costume editor and make it shorter. I have selected the second method i.e. to reduce the size of line sprite in costume editor.

QR CODE TO THE GAME AND CODE.

Scan the code using your mobile or open the link :

https://scratch.mit.edu/projects/508875810

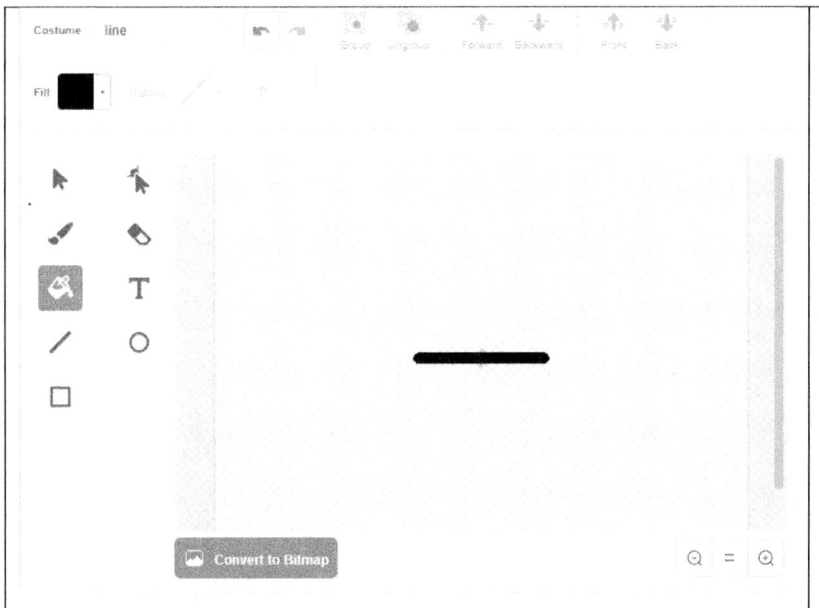

Just select the sprite "line" and go to its costumes. You will find the larger image of the costume with an editor. Click on the "Convert to Bitmap" button, edit your sprite and convert it back to vector after editing.

It is as simple as you are working in MS Paint software of windows.

Moving the paddle

Before we set in other stuff, we need to move the paddle. We have two options, one is to move the paddle with arrow keys. The second option is to move the paddle with the mouse. I select the second option to move the paddle with the mouse.

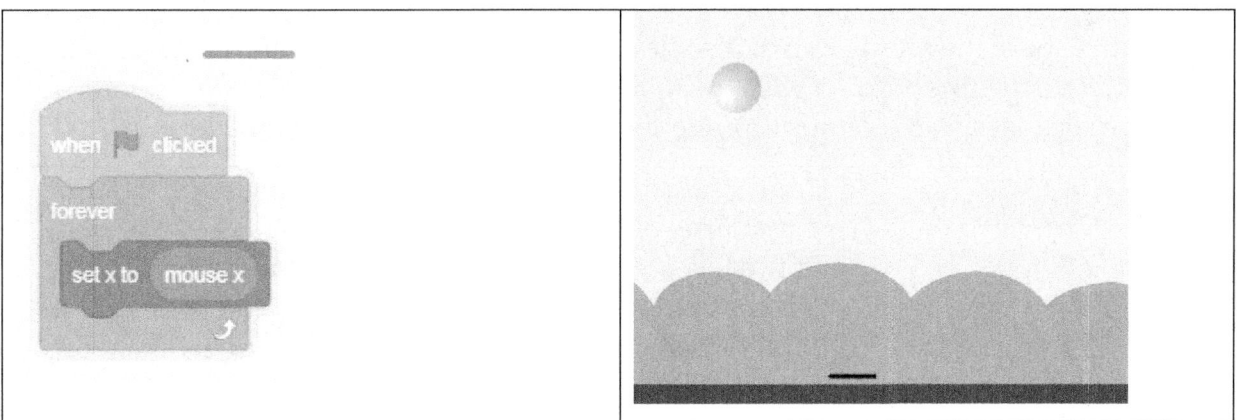

The code for moving paddle is very simple, the first code block is to start the code when the flag is clicked. The second block is to repeat this forever. This is done so that the paddle keeps moving according to the mouse till the code is not stopped.

The only code line that moves the paddle is "set x to mouse x". This code block can be found in motion categories as "set x to -200". An example is shown below:

	Here, you can change the value of x such that the location of the paddle can be moved right or left.

You already know that paddle has an x and y location on the screen. If we drag the paddle on the screen and set them as per our requirement the value of x and y are visible in the sprite window. The example is shown below:

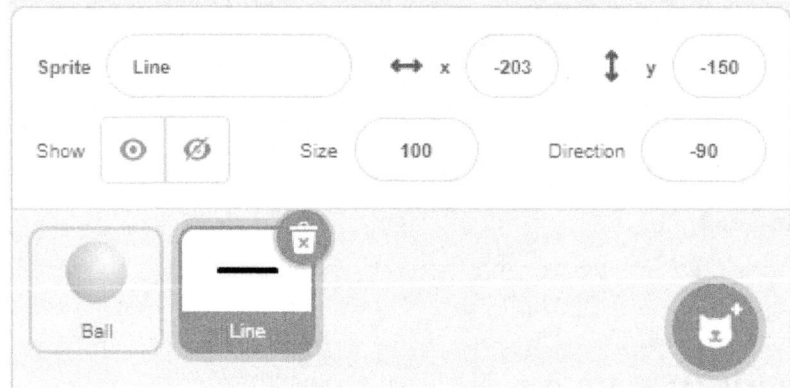

Changing the value of x to some other value will move the paddle horizontally, either the left or right. The "Set x to ____" code block means to change the value of x of sprite while keeping the value of y unchanged. It is similar to the "goto" statement wherein the value of y is not changing.

Similar to the sprite the mouse cursor also have x and y value to define its location on the screen. We have to link sprite's x with the mouse's cursor's x value. For this purpose, you can explore section sensing for appropriate code to get the value of the mouse.

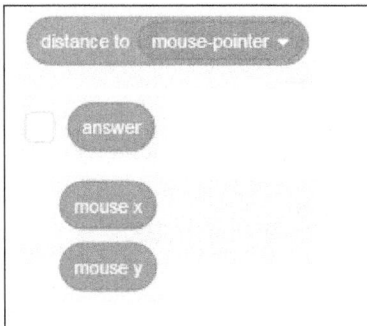	Under the sensing category, we have few blocks relating to a mouse. Also, note the shape of each block over here. Only a few are oval. The "set x to " block has an oval shape to accept a value of x, so we can only select an oval-shaped block. Therefore, we will only focus on oval-shaped blocks. The most appropriate is "mouse x". Drag this mouse x block and fit it into the oval shape of the "Set x to" block.

Now, whatever is the horizontal value of the mouse's pointer i.e. x value, the same will become x value for the paddle. If we move the mouse, the paddle will also move. You can run the code and check the development done so far.

Bouncing Ball from the paddle

Before we make code for a bouncing ball, we must understand and learn about conditional code blocks. These type of code statements falls under the category of control flow. Normally, codes are executed from top to bottom. Control flow statements break up the flow of statement execution by decision making, repeating, and branching, enabling the script to conditionally execute a particular set of statements. There are majorly two types of control flow statements - one for repeating certain tasks/statements i.e. the loop statement that we have already covered. The type of loop statements that we have already encountered are "forever loop" or repeat to execute the block of code after loop block for a certain number of times.

The other set of statements are to branch off flow leading to skipping of certain statements or execution of certain statements depending on the conditions.

The examples of conditional code blocks are given below :

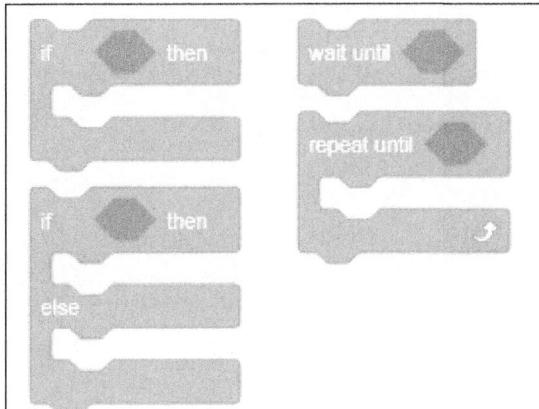	The two most commonly used blocks are "if-then" and "if-then-else" blocks. The block codes between the arms of conditional block statements after the "then" statement are executed only if the condition in a hexagonal box (a box with six sides) is true. While code block after "else block" is executed only if the condition in the hexagonal box is not true.

To make it simple, assume you need some answers from the animation window like is sprite one touching another sprite or any other question whose answer is in the form of yes or no and not in the form of a numerical value, then you can use "if.. then" or if… then …else" conditional block statement.

A typical example is my ball touches the paddle then there will be bounce else no bounce. So, "the ball touches the paddle" is my condition which when becomes "yes" the bounce code written in between arms of if block after "then" will get executed.

We also know that the condition for the ball touching paddle should be a hexagonal code block. We can search this block in event or sensing categories of code blocks. In the sensing, we have the following major hexagonal-shaped code blocks.

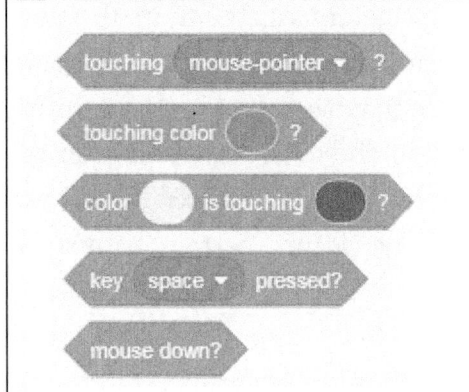

Since the action of bounce is on the ball after touching, the code is to be written for the ball sprite.

The first code block that we have is "touching mouse-pointer". The drop-down menu also provides the name of the paddle sprite i.e. line. Therefore this code of block can be used in the if block statement.

The second code of block "touching color" can also be used The paddle color is different from all other colors including the background, I can use this block of statement. When the ball touches a particular color, i.e. the color of the paddle the ball should bounce. The sprite touching a color will only work perfectly if the color is unique on the screen and the color is not shared by any other sprite or background. Here, my paddle is black and none of the sprite or background is using this color so I can also use this block of code.

The third option is to use "color___ is touching ___ ?". This block of code will only work if both the colors are unique on the screen and no other sprite or background shares these two colors. This can also be used here, as the ball color is yellow and the paddle color is black and the background does not use any of these colors.

We can use any of these three blocks of code, I will be using the first one here. You can drag the code block and put it into hexagonal space provided after "if" in the code block, they will get fit with each other. You can observe that all the hexagonal-shaped code blocks ask a question and the answer for these questions are in the form of "yes" or "no".

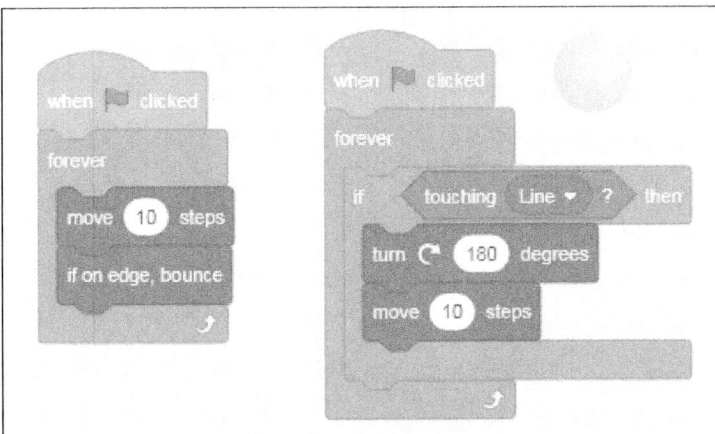

This block of code would be written separately under the ball sprite as the action is on the part of the ball. If you write this code block of bouncing under the paddle, the paddle will bounce after touching the ball.

Why the code has been written separately and not below the existing code for bouncing off the edges? This could have two answers, the forever loop does not have a hook to allow attachment of further block of codes. This is a crude answer, the real answer is that the forever loop is running continuously forever. We also know that codes are executed from top to bottom. If forever code is running forever, then the code blocks below forever will never get a chance to get executed.

The code for bouncing when the ball touches the paddle is to turn the direction 180 degree and move 10 steps. The 180-degree means sending back the ball to the direction from which it came. You can run the code and see that this type of bounce sometimes makes repetitive bounces on the screen and the game will not be challenging. Now it is time to understand direction before we move ahead.

Understanding Direction

The direction of any sprite can be noted from the sprite window after selecting the sprite. The direction can have a value from 0 to 360 degrees. Direction is always measured in degrees. For your understanding, you can assume that you have a rocket as a sprite with its nose upward and reading on direction window of the sprite is 90.

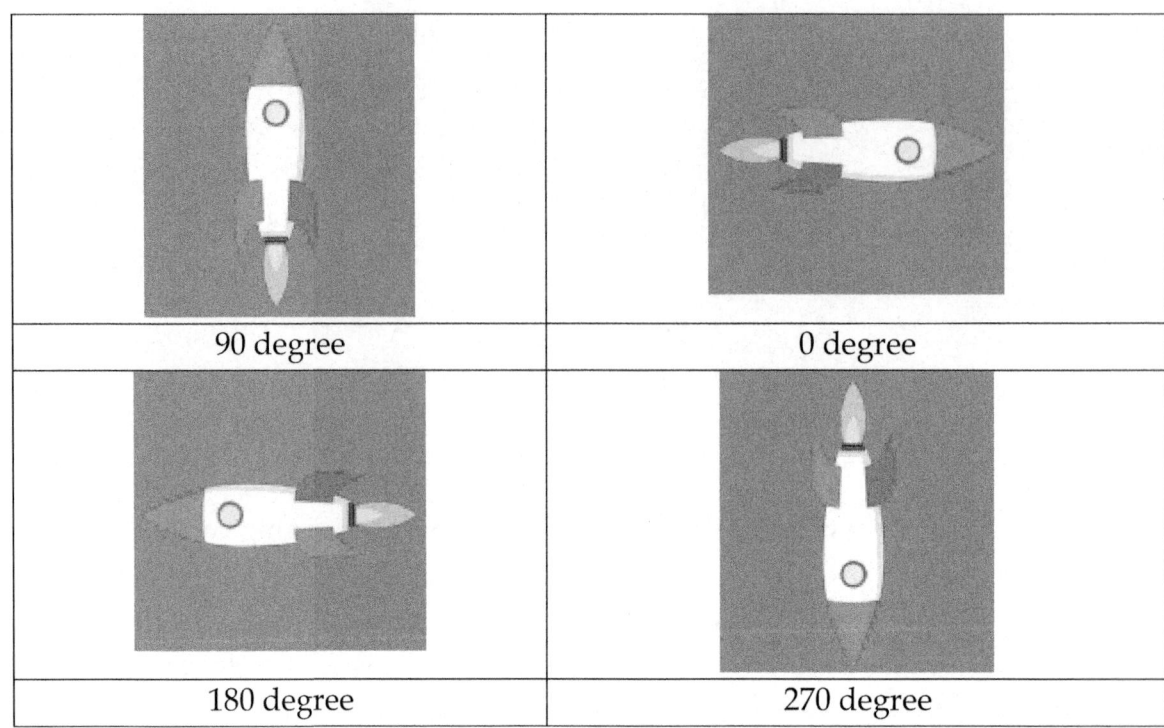

90 degree	0 degree
180 degree	270 degree

Any horizontal position of a rocket would be +/- 90 degrees of the upward direction. Rocket with the right direction would be -90 degree and rocket with position left would be +90 degree.

To help you remembering directions, look at the diagram below:

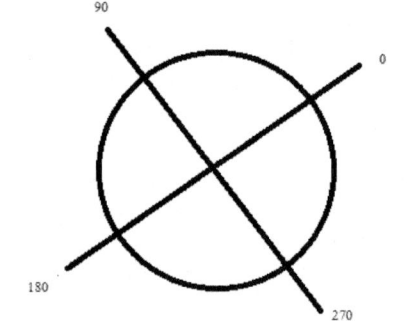	If any direction, whether it is the top or left side, right side, or any direction is marked as zero, then just the opposite side would be 180 degrees. Let's assume you are standing facing a mirror and I mark that direction as zero, then the 180-degree direction would be when you rotate yourself left or right in such a way that now your back is facing the mirror.
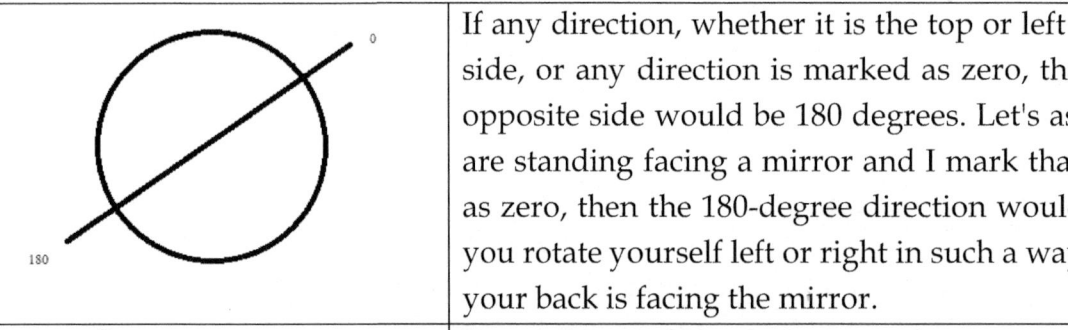	For making a 180 rotation, you have to exactly move half-circle standing at your place. The other two directions when your left and right shoulders were facing mirrors were 90 degrees and 270 degrees. Direction. You may note that 90 is the middle point of 0 and 180 degrees and the angle exactly opposite to 90 should be 90 +180.

| 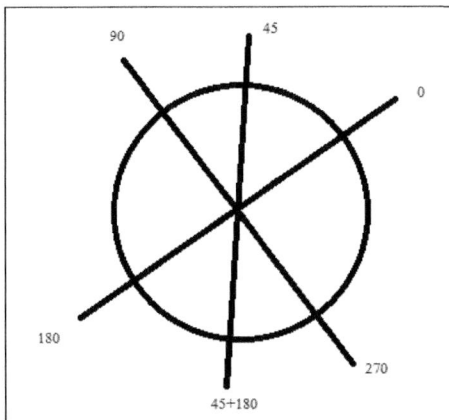 | In nutshell moving one-fourth of a full round standing at one place is either +90 degree or -90 degree. Other angles in between can thus be found. Also, remember that one full round is 360 degrees. If you are standing facing a mirror and you rotate at you own place, one full round, then it is 360 degree. Moving one-fourth right to 0 degree is therefore 360-90 = 270 degrees. |

If you find the above concept difficult, leave it for now and take the help of the direction tool in the sprite window. Anyway, these angles are part of your maths classes, if you have not learned them now you can learn them in your maths classes.

Now, our problem was that we were bouncing the ball back at 180 degrees and this was creating a predictive move, which could be repetitive in some cases. This was also making over game simple and less challenging. If we change the bounce angle any value automatically generated by the computer our work will be done. But, this may create another problem of bouncing the ball from the paddle to below paddles.

The workable solution is therefore to select any angle which is nearer to 180 to avoid repeating bounces. Let us make it any value in between 160 to 200 degrees. Any value is called random. There is a code block to do this.

| `pick random 1 to 10` | This code block can be located in the operator category of blocks. |

This code block generates a random value between two values provided to it. Here in our case, those two values will be 160 and 200.

The last code block is thus changed as under :

The old code block	The changed code block
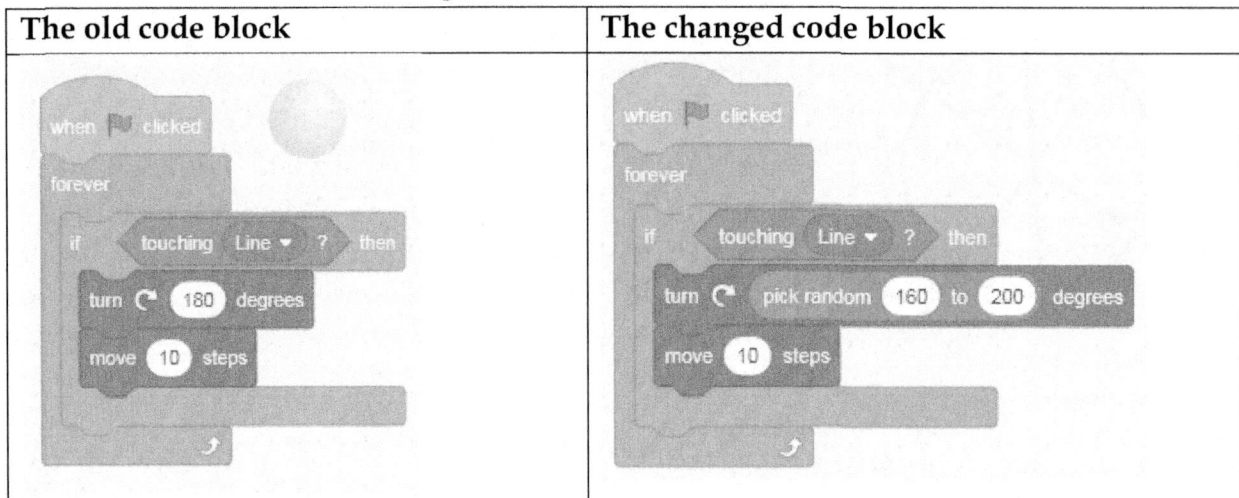	

Game end coding

The game would end when the ball misses the peddle and falls. How to code this part? Let us have a look at the background I selected.

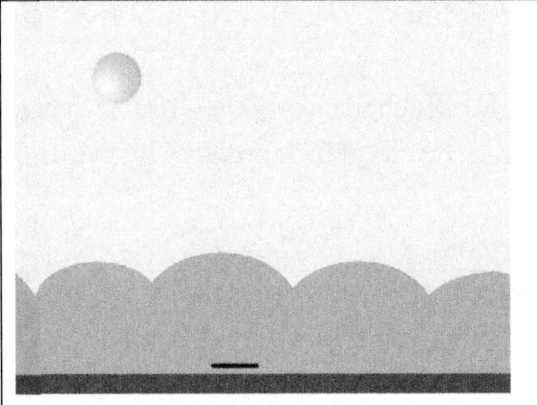 Below the paddle line, I have a dark brown line. Touching the ball with a dark brown line can be used for the ending game.

We will need to ask a question to the script "is the ball touching the baseline" and the answer will be as yes or no. We have already studied that such types of answers are generated by hexagonal (six-sided) code blocks. Further, this coding will be conditional because, if the condition is not true, the game will continue else the game will stop.

With this, we already know that we need to use the "if.. then" code block and Hexa code block from the sensing category.

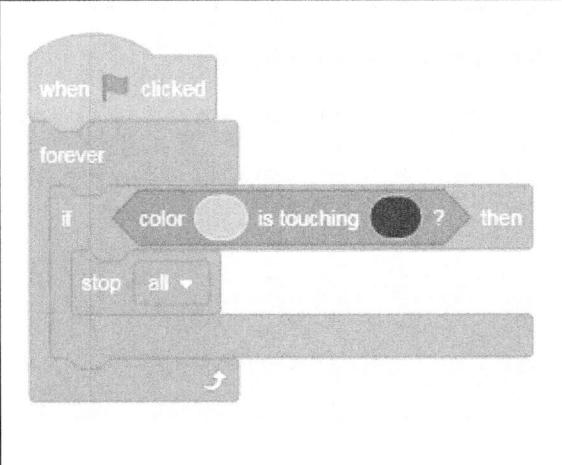	This code has been written for ball sprite as the ball and background will be interacting in this part. It again starts from when flag clicked block as other two blocks for ball i.e. bouncing from edges and to bounce from paddle are in forever loop. Here again, we will always keep looking for the interaction of the ball with the bottom line of the background, we are using a forever loop.

We have taken the "if-then" block from controls and sensing block of one color touching another color. You can click color to change the color inside the block to a ball color.

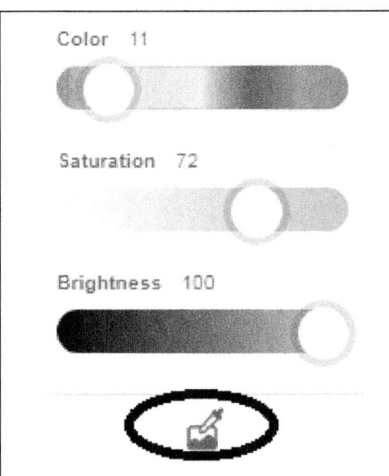	Select the color picker from the bottom and click on the ball in the animation window. This will select the color of the ball for you. Similarly, for the second color, click on the color and this window will open for you. Now select the color picker from the bottom as indicated in the image and select the bottom dark brown border of the background.

Inside the if-then block just drag and drop the "stop all" code block from controls and this will end the animation of all the sprites in the game.

End Game Screen

You can run the code till this point. The ball will bounce from the edges and paddle. If you fail to control the ball on the run, drag and put the ball sprite at the top edge. This will provide you some time to react and control the ball.

As soon as you fail to control the ball, the ball would fall on the bottom dark brown line of the background and everything will come to a halt. This is the end of the game.

How the game should end?

The game should not end without any message to its user. It should have at least told you that the game is over.

Let us create another sprite with the message "Game Over". Since the "game over" sprite is not available in the sprite library, we have to make this sprite ourselves. You have two options for making this sprite, either use any photo editing tool to make a "game over" message as a transparent image file. Photoshop is a good tool to create transparent images, however, you can also use the built-in tool provided in the scratch platform.

In the sprite window, click the add sprite sign. Click on the "paint" button. This will open up the image editing tool similar to MS paint of windows. Use the text tool to type Game Over or any other message. Use the selection tool to select the entire message, now drag the same to the center of the screen.

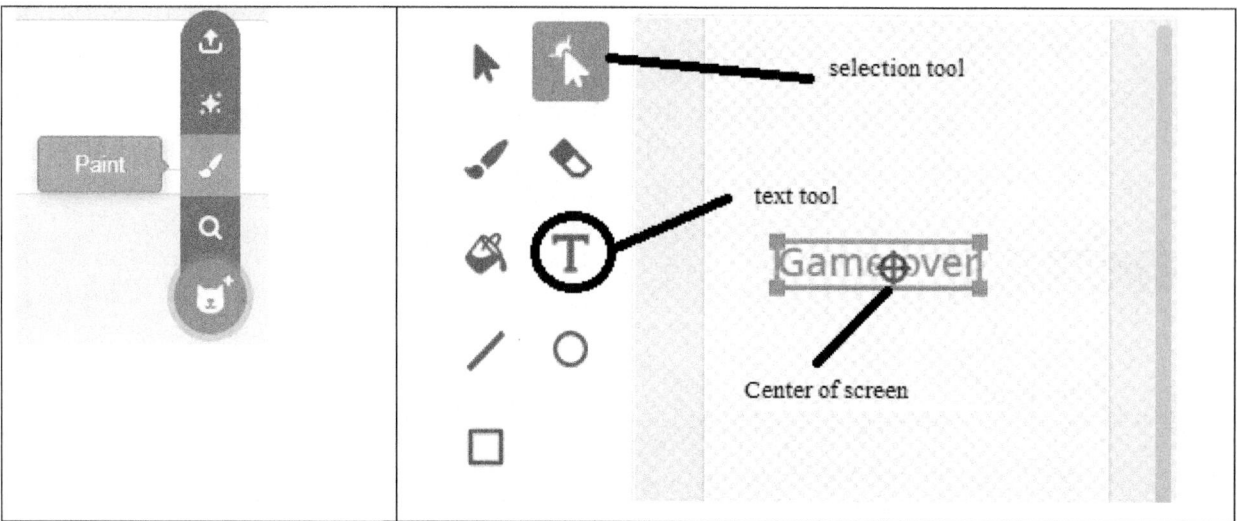

This will create another sprite in the sprite window. Now, the problem is that even at the start of the game, the game over sprite is appearing. I need to hide this sprite at the start of the game and only show it at the end of the game. How can I do this?

Broadcast Message

Here comes the role of another important code block that can be found under the category of the event. The code blocks are

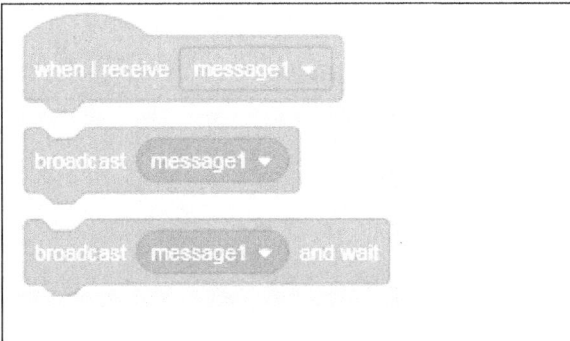	When you click the flag button all the sprites start to work. If you want to say stop one sprite for a while another sprite is working or to ask other sprites to work when an event has occurred in the game. You would be required to communicate between two sprites.

For communicating between two sprites we use messages. The message sending sprite will use the "broadcast message" block and the message receiving sprite will use the "when I receive message" block.

I need to hide this sprite at the start of the game and only show it at the end of the game. For doing this, I will need two small code blocks.

	Both of these code blocks can be located under the "looks" category.

As the name suggests, the "show" block will make the sprite visible on the screen, and the "hide" code block will make the block invisible on-screen.

Now, I will make a code to hide the sprite at the beginning of the game.

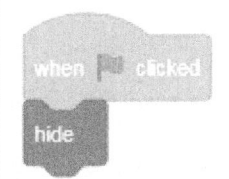	The code block will be added to the "Game Over" sprite as the action to get hide is on its part. The code is simple, on clicking the start button, the Game Over sprite will get itself hide.

Now when will it know that it's time to get unhide and show itself. This information can only be obtained from the game over code which is on the ball sprite. This means ball sprite has to tell some message to the Game Over sprite. Therefore, we will add a code to broadcast messages to Game Over Code. The code blocks before and after adding the broadcast message code block are shown below.

The old code block	The changed code block
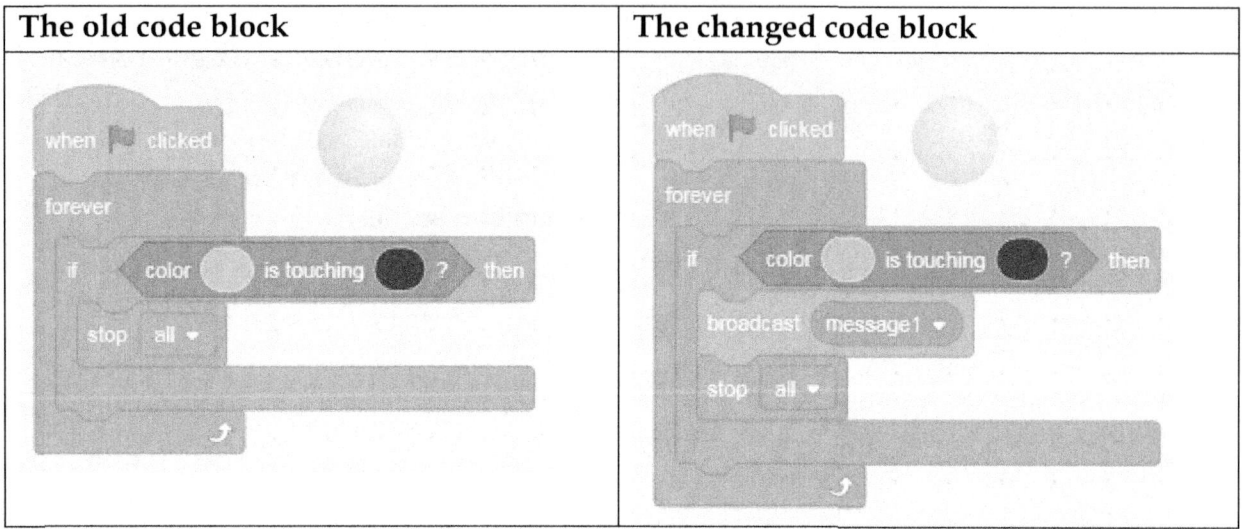	

The broadcast message by the name message1 is available to all sprite in the project. Any of the sprites are allowed to receive a message. The show itself action will be on the part of the "Game Over" sprite, therefore message receiving code and show code will be written in the "Game Over" sprite.

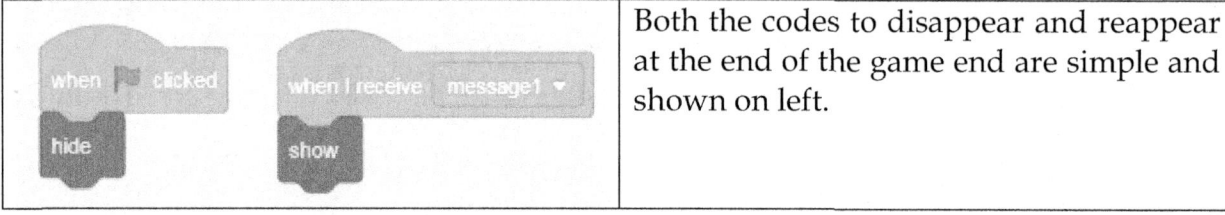	Both the codes to disappear and reappear at the end of the game end are simple and shown on left.

The result of the code will be game over the window at the end of the game as shown here:

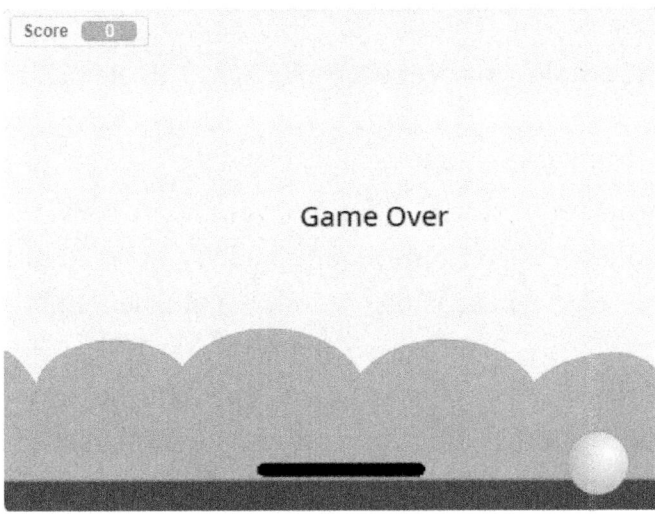

Adding Score

No game is complete without scores to measure performance and to compare scores with our friends. In the last window of a game over, there is a score on the left top corner. The score is displayed here. For each bounce from the ball from the paddle, the score is increased by one point.

For calculating and storing a value for a score, a variable is required. Now, what is this variable?

In nature, we have various objects and materials and we have different ways to store them. In the kitchen, I keep oil and water in bottles, grain in containers, or bags. When I work from home, I save my data in a pen drive. You would agree that bags, bottles, containers, and pen drives are all storage devices. In case, I am unable to locate my pen drive, can I save my data in a bottle. Can I save kitchen oil in the pen drive? Should I save my grain in a bottle? Probably your answer is no. I cannot save kitchen oil in a pen drive and data in a bottle. My question is why I cannot save kitchen oil in pen drive?

Each object has some specific characteristics. Oil is liquid they require a different type of storage container than grains. Depending on the properties of the object we choose a method for their storage.

Similarly, in computer language, we have information of various types, and such information is stored based on the type of data or piece of information it contains. Information to be stored may have :

1. The numbers, like whole numbers example: 1, 2, 3, 4, etc or decimal numbers.
2. We may also have names like James, Kitty, Dolly, Rosy, Ammie these names or any alphanumeric are known as string
3. Some of the information is stored in form of yes and no only. Such type of information is known as "Boolean" in computer language. We have already seen that the results of hexagonal code blocks in sensing are in form of true and false.

For each of the above types of information that we may require, different types of containers or information holders to store. The classification of information by its type is called datatype. We may, therefore, three data types in scratch.

DataType	Example
NUMBERS	509, 430.6, 600
STRING	Ammie, JOJO, 500MG
BOOLEAN	TRUE or FALSE

Scratch has a shape for each of the three above types of data. Boolean variables and values have hexagonal shapes (six sides,) while numbers and strings have oval-shaped code blocks. We have already seen all of them

A Variable is a container to store information. Variable can be of any data type as per your requirement. It could be number, string, boolean. Variable can store information, it can be emptied, rewritten, and reused as many times as you require.

Here we require a variable for storage of score value. We are required to give a name to the variable for its identification before we use it. Generally, programmers provide a name to variables that are easy to remember and provide ideas to coders about the information that it is storing. I can give the name "Score" or "Points" or anything at my convenience.

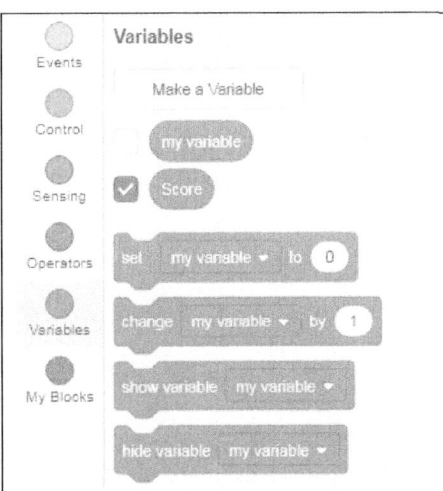

Select the "variable" category and click on "Make a variable". Clicking this will allow you to select a name for the variable, I have selected score as the name of a variable and selected "for all sprites".

This will create a new variable as a score.

Inside the code where the ball touches paddle and bounces back add the code block. "change score by 1" from the variable set of code blocks. This will increase the score by 1 every time, the ball touches the paddle.

The complete set of code is shown here:

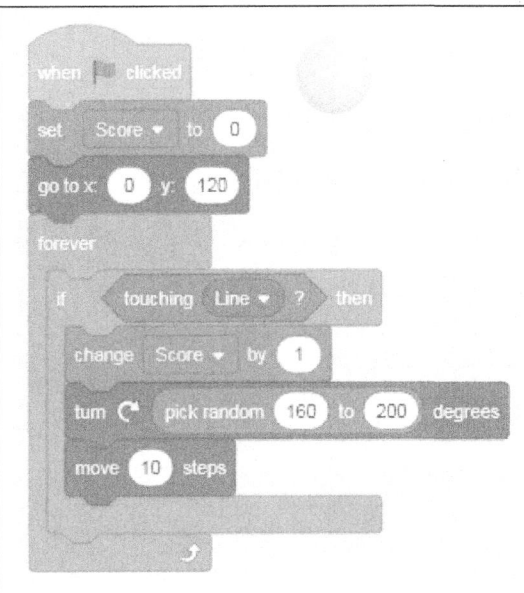

When the first-time game starts, the score is set to zero, otherwise, the earlier score will keep on continuing.

We set the ball at the top edge before starting the game so that the player gets enough time to react.

The third change to the last code block is that we have added the code block to change the score by 1 after the ball touches the line sprite.

The Entire Code

The ball sprite code

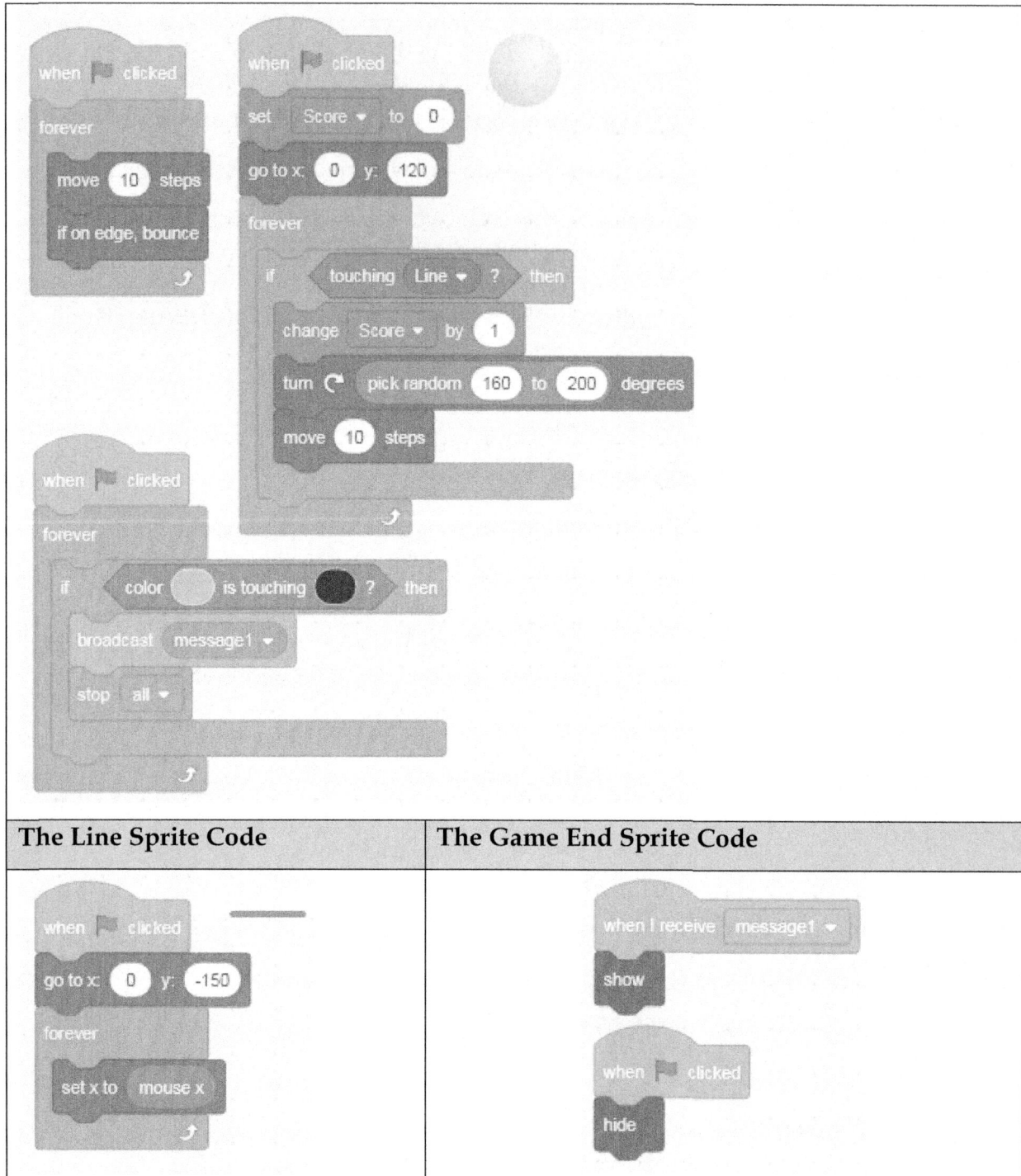

Chapter-6: Simple Baseball Game

Based on the knowledge gained so far, we will make a simple baseball game. All the sprite and background are available in the scratch library.

The ball will be bowled by the computer every 5 seconds. By clicking the batsman will try to hit the ball. If the color of the ball touches the color of the bat, the ball will turn 45 degrees and will bounce away and the score will be increased by 1, else the score will be reduced by one. If you leave the ball, there will be neither deduction of score nor score will increase. This is a fairly simple game to play. We have learned all the required skills to make this game. You are encouraged to try it out yourself.

	**Scan QR Code to open Simple Baseball Game or go to the link https://scratch.mit.edu/projects/509604859**

Sprites Required

The sprites required are the ball and the batter. The background of the stage may be selected as per you. Arrange all the sprites at their position as per the image shown on the first page of the chapter.

Bowling

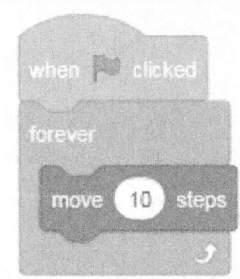	This will move the ball by 10 steps forever. It requires some more modification because if the ball gets past the screen it will get disappear.
	There are only two conditions when the ball will get past the edges 1. When the batsman misses the ball and 2. When the batsman hits the ball.
	In both cases, the ball is required to be reset to its initial position.
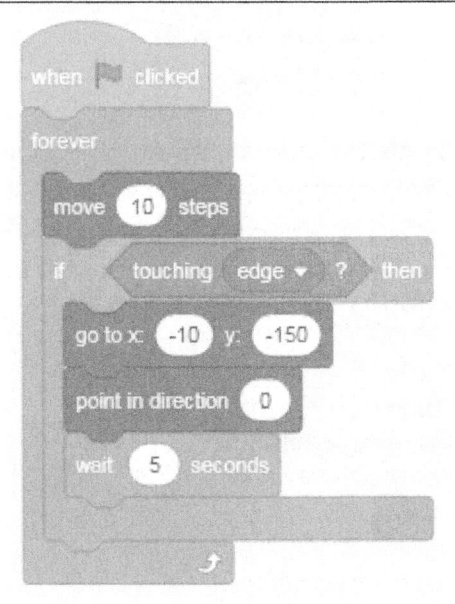	If the ball touches the edge, the ball is reset to its initial position, i.e. x=-10 and y=-150. The direction of the ball is also set to 0 so that on move 10 steps, the ball moves in the upward direction only. After the batsman hits the ball, the direction of the ball is changed, and not setting the direction to 0 will let the ball move in some other direction than the desired direction.
	The last code is "wait 5 seconds", this is added to let the batsman get ready for the next bowling. If you feel that the time is more you may reduce it to 3 or 4 seconds.

Batsman's action

The batsman has four costumes for complete action. We can either assign a key for the batsman's action or may use a mouse click as an event to start the batsman's action. The action of the batsman can be created by changing all the four costumes of the batsman in quick succession. Here we have two codes that do the same work, the second code block is shorter as it has used a repeat block of code to remove repetition of the next costume and "wait for block" of code.

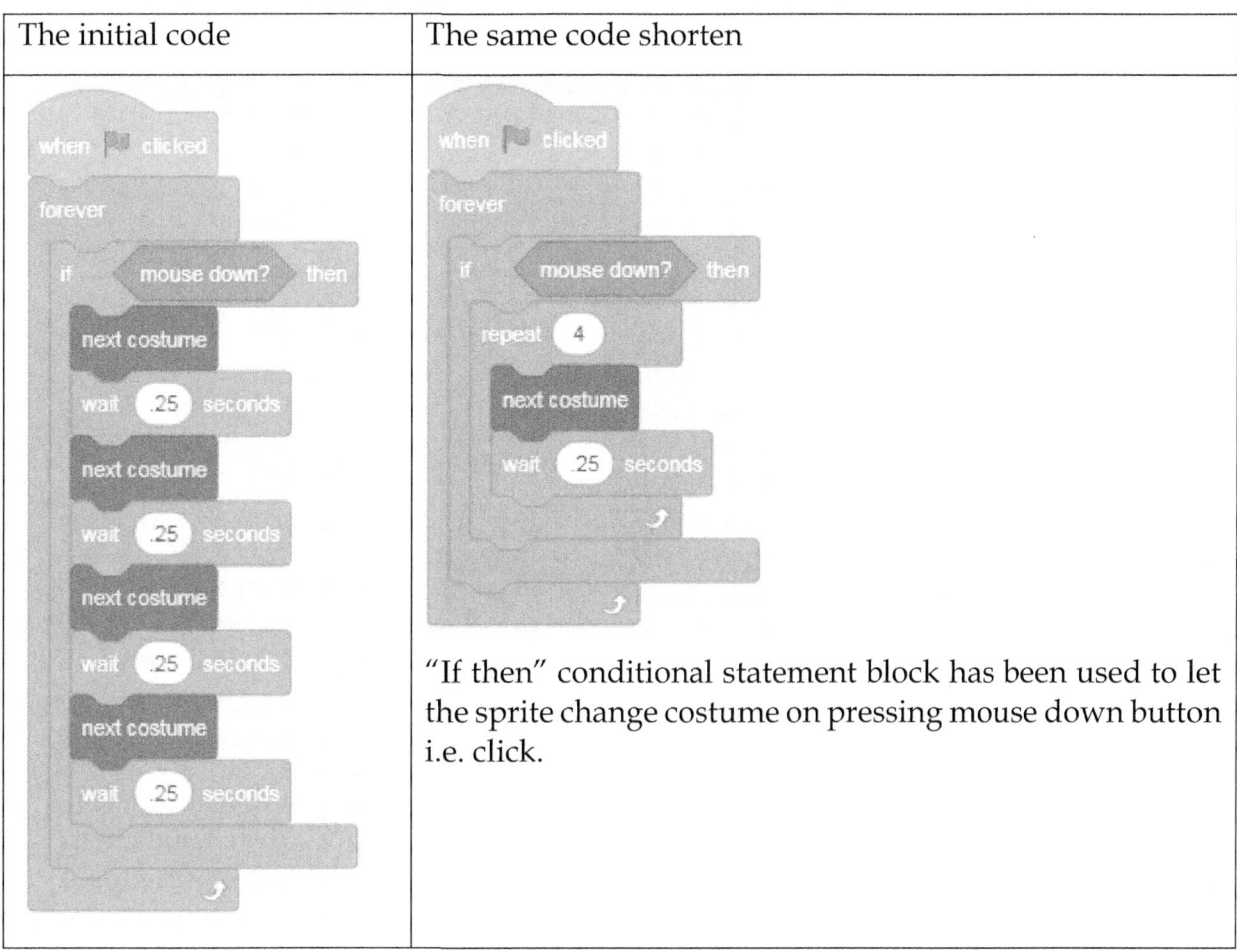

The initial code	The same code shorten
	"If then" conditional statement block has been used to let the sprite change costume on pressing mouse down button i.e. click.

You may run the code for the two sprites. You will notice that the ball is released every 5 secs and on clicking the mouse button, the bat's man moves his bat to hit the ball. You know what will be our next set of codes. You will code such that when the color of the ball touches the color of the bat, the ball moves by some degrees and goes away. Make sure that the ball is aligned in the line of the bat shot.

Shot on ball

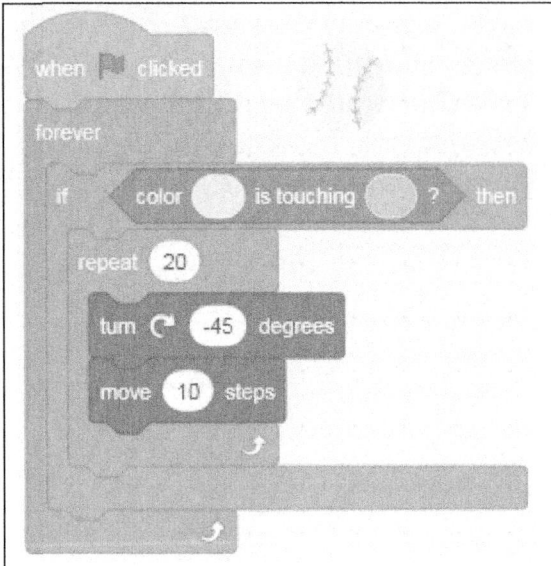

This code will be on the ball sprite as the action of bounce will be on ball.

The bounce code will turn the angle by 45 degrees 20 times creating a spiral movement and then move 10 steps.

The entire code is in forever block, because the system will have to look every second and every millisecond for the condition that the color of the ball is touching the color of the bat.

Score Keeping

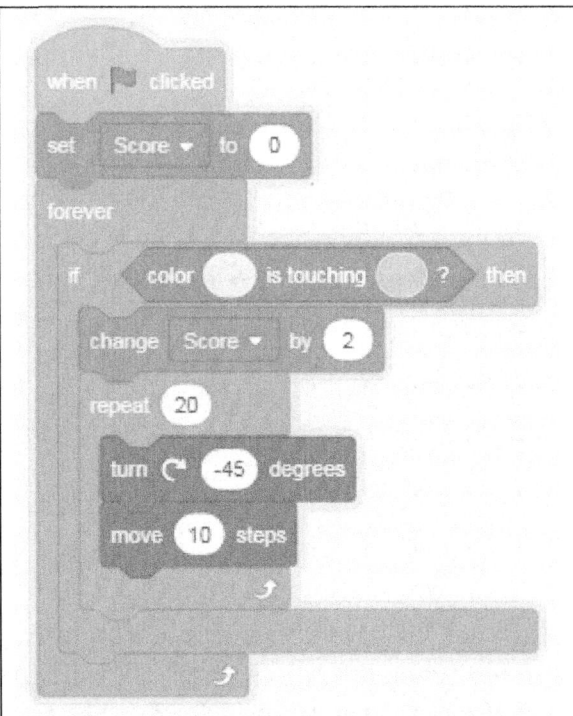

The rule for scores are as follows :

1. If you miss the ball, one score will be deducted
2. If you hit the ball, one score will be added. All hit ball goes out of the edge so you get -1, therefore you should add +2 to increase the score.

As soon as the start button is clicked, it sets the score as zero. Here is that code to increase score by one on the ball being hit by the ball.

Similarly, put code to deduct one mark on being at the edge. Both the codes will be for ball sprite.

The Entire Code

Here is the entire code for you.

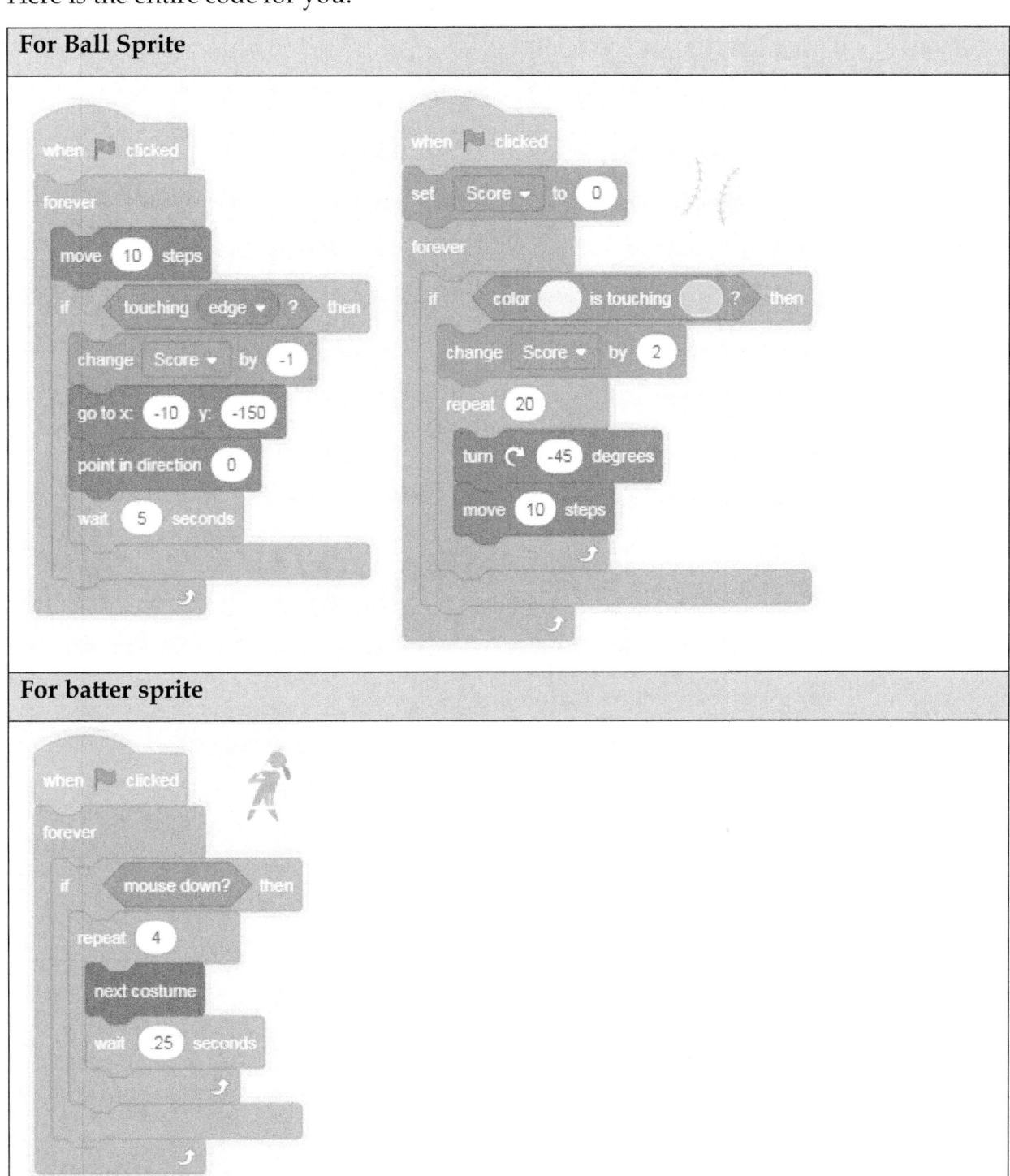

Chapter-7: Balloon Burst Game

The objective of this game is to make to familiar with custom sprite i.e. a sprite that is not available in the library of scratch and use of size code block to change the size of the sprite.

The game is to burst the balloon by bringing the mouse cursor over the balloon. If the cursor is too near to the balloon, the balloon will move to a random position. If you are fast enough to bring the cursor on the balloon will make a pop sound and a pop animation get produce.

An image of the game is shown below :

The game can be accessed at the below-mentioned web address.

	**You can either scan the QR code or visit the link https://scratch.mit.edu/projects/510137880** to play the game.

Required of Sprites

A balloon sprite is required and a pop image is required. The pop image will be uploaded as a costume of the sprite. The balloon sprite is available in the scratch sprite library, however, unfortunately, the pop image or pop sprite is not available. You can search "balloon pop" image from google. Make sure that the image you download is transparent. As regard background, you may select any one that you like.

Transparent image

A transparent image allows the background to be shown around the image. If the image is not transparent the background around the image will be shown as a black or white color. An example is shown below.

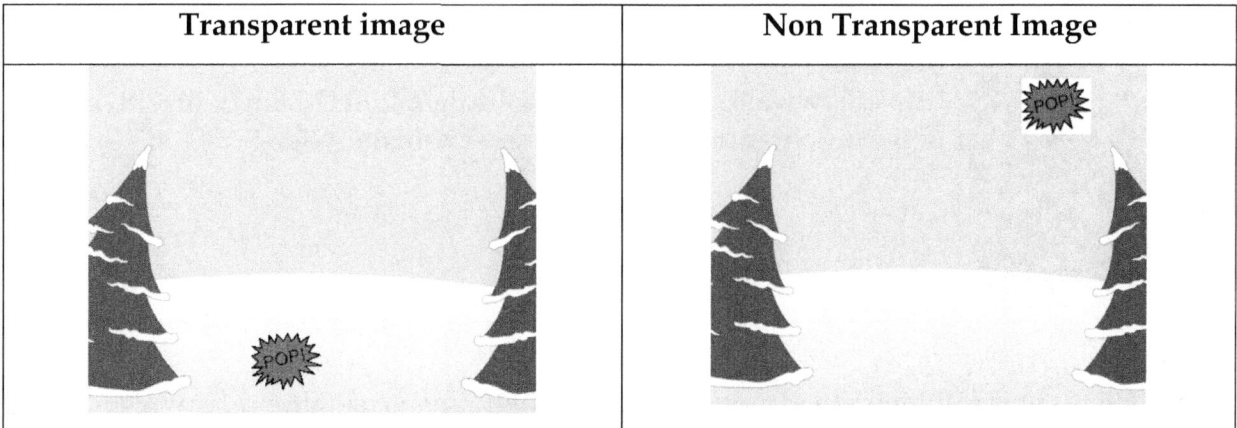

The file extension of images are generally .gif, .jpeg, .jpg,.bmp and png. The only format that can preserve a transparent image is .png. Any transparent image when saved in a format other than .png will become a non-transparent image,

Searching transparent image on google images

In google search for balloon pop. Make sure you search them in images and not under all categories. Once the results appear, you can filter the results of balloon pop by clicking on the tool and then under the color category select "transparent".

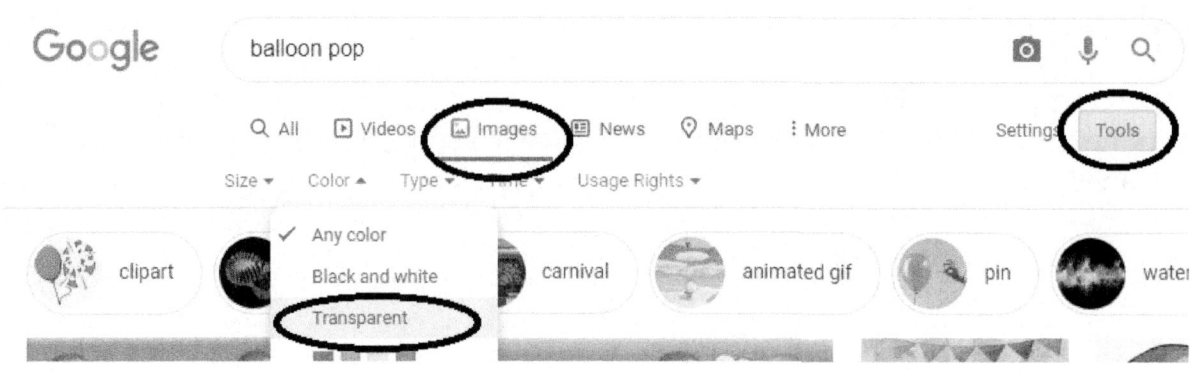

This will provide you results of all the transparent images with balloon pop.

Under the category, you can select any of the images that fit your requirement. After, a search, I have selected the image which is available below URL:

	You can either scan the QR code or can download it directly for this URL https://www.clipartmax.com/middle/m2i8H7G6m2G6H7i8_balloon-pop-clip-art-at-clker-clip-art-explosion-sign/

If you like, you may also download any other transparent image of balloon pop from google and save it in PNG format. Make sure to note the name of the image and the location where you saved your image. I renamed the image pop and saved it on the desktop of my windows computer.

Adding an image as Costume

Select balloon sprite from the sprite window and click on the costume button for the balloon. You will find that balloon is already having three costumes that allow it to change color.

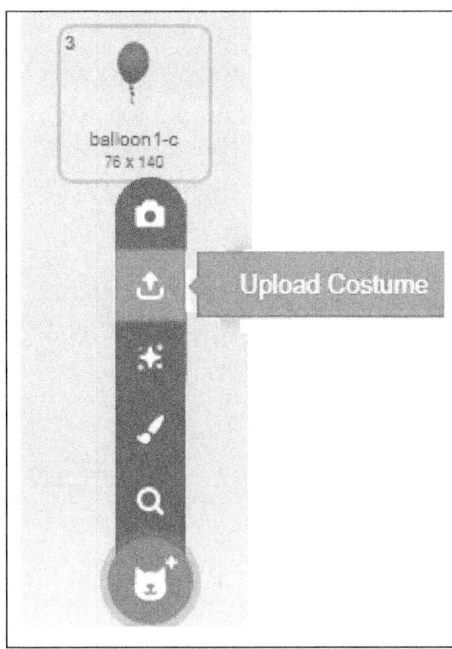

Click on the plus sign at the bottom of the costume window and select the upload costume button as shown in the image on the left.

This will open a window to let you select the image of the new costume. Select the image you just downloaded. In my case, I have selected a pop image from the desktop.

After upload, click on the pop image and the image will get displayed on the animation screen.

The size of the pop is larger than the balloon size. It seems that we may need to reduce the size of the pop for use.

Moving balloon randomly on the screen

The below code blocks are required to be added to the balloon sprite. Since we are required to ask a question from the animation itself, we may use "if code block"

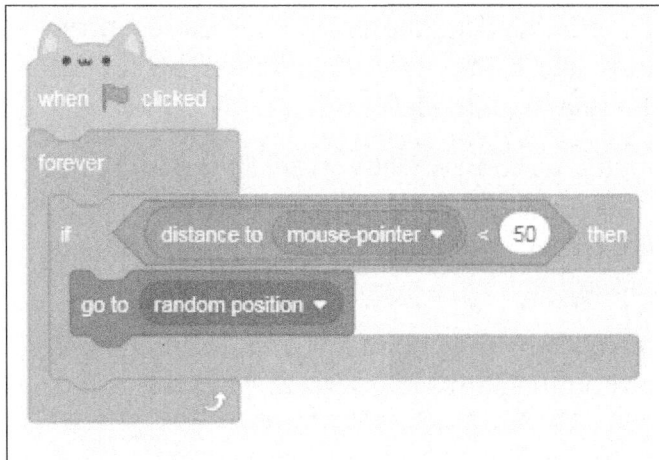

As the game starts, every time (forever) the code block "if the distance to mouse-pointer<50 then" will check for the condition. The condition is "whether the distance of mouse pointer and balloon is less than 50?"

We already know that the screen is from about -200 to +200. A distance of 50 is a small distance.

You can find the if block from the control set of blocks. The "distance to mouse-pointer" block can be located under a sensing set of the block of codes. You can notice that the "if..then" block accepts a hexagonal (six-sided) block of code and the answer it accepts, is in the form of yes and no only. The distance to the mouse pointer is a round block of code and it provides value and not the answer in form of yes or no. The two cannot fit together. Further, we need to check if the distance from the mouse pointer is less than 50, therefor we need another code of the block.

Select operator block set of code and locate, the below operator block.

On the other side of round space to put a block, place distance to mouse-pointer block. This will for the code block as under :

Now this entire block of code is a hexagonal block of code (the block with six sides). We can put this block in if block. The question asked from the animation is "is the distance of balloon and mouse-pointer less than 50", if the answer is no, we will do nothing, and if the answer is yes the code block between the arms of if block will get executed.

The code block between the arms of the if block is "goto random position". This code is written under balloon sprite, the action will be taken by balloon, and the balloon will move to a random location.

Some of you might get a pop image instead of a balloon image on the first run and on bringing a mouse pointer nearer to the pop image the pop image will move to a random location on the screen. This is because the balloon now has four costumes and the costume selected from the costume window would be available on the screen.

This problem can be solved by making balloon-a (the first costume) as a costume on the first run. The revised code only requires putting "switch costume to balloon1-a" code block between when flag clicked code block and forever block.

You can run this code and check whether the same is working as intended. On bringing the mouse pointer nearer to the balloon the balloon should move to a new unknown location on the screen.

POP the Balloon

The plan is that when the mouse pointer touches the balloon, a pop sound would get produce and the balloon image would change to a pop image.

The action for changing the costume is since on the part of the balloon the entire code should be written under balloon sprite.

Further, it will be a separate code of block as other code we wrote had a forever loop and it will not allow adding another code below it.

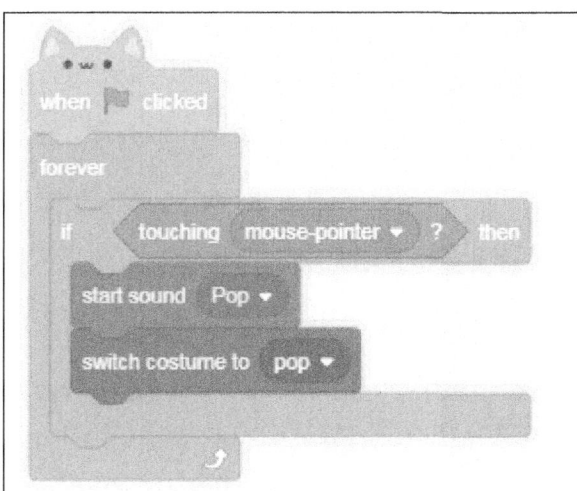	This code will also start with the start of the animation, so the first code block is "when the flag is clicked"
	We will regularly, every second of the time will look for and ask animation whether the mouse pointer is touching the balloon. So, we will be using another forever block. As a thumb rule for use of any sensor-related block code, we are required to use a forever loop.

Now, we will ask the animation a question of whether the mouse pointer is touching the balloon. The answer to this question will be provided by animation in the form of yes or no, therefore we must use "if code of block". If the answer is no, we will do nothing, and if the answer is yes, the code block in the arms of if block will get executed.

Needless to say that, touching the mouse-pointer block is available under the sensing set of the block of codes.

Under the sound block code, you can find the start sound pop block and you can change the costume of the balloon to pop by use of the "switch costume to pop" code block.

Now start the game, note the issues with the game.

1. The size of the pop costume is very large.
2. After the pop image is generated, the balloon image is not shown. We are not switching to the balloon image.

Solving issues

The first problem can be solved by adding "set size to " code block from the "looks" category of blocks to reduce the size of the pop costume. Now, we need to change the costume back to the balloon costume after the pop has been done.

In between the switch of costume from pop to balloon costume, we should use wait code block for waiting so that we can see pop costume before it is quickly switched back to balloon costume.

The solution ode is the below code :

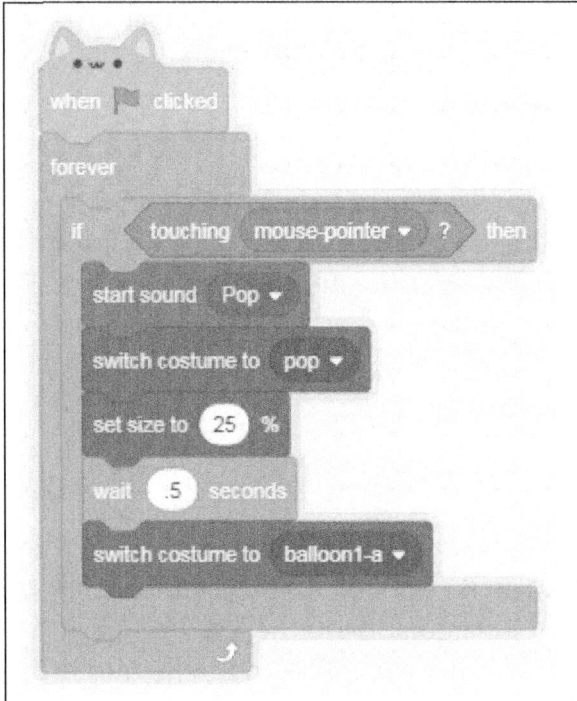

After, "switch costume to pop", we make the size 25 % i.e. smaller, and will wait for half second and will again have a balloon costume.

I Hope, this would solve all the problems and the game will run as intended.

You may require to run codes many times and note problems or errors and correct them. No expert can make any game or program in a single go without testing and correcting the problems.

Now run the code. Some of the problems have been solved but new problems have emerged.

The problem that I can notice is that the size of the balloon after pop has also reduced. This error can quickly be corrected by using a code block "set size to 100 %" after the "switch costume to balloon1-a" code block.

Now, again run the game and play the game. Are there any more issues? I can see one more issue that after the pop it again becomes a balloon and since the cursor is on the balloon, the balloon again gets popped. If you are unable to understand the problem, you have to run the code to understand the problem. There is a need to move to another location before the balloon switches the costume. This can be easily done by adding a "goto random position" code block.

The entire code block for the balloon is given in the next section

The Entire Code

Balloon Sprite Code

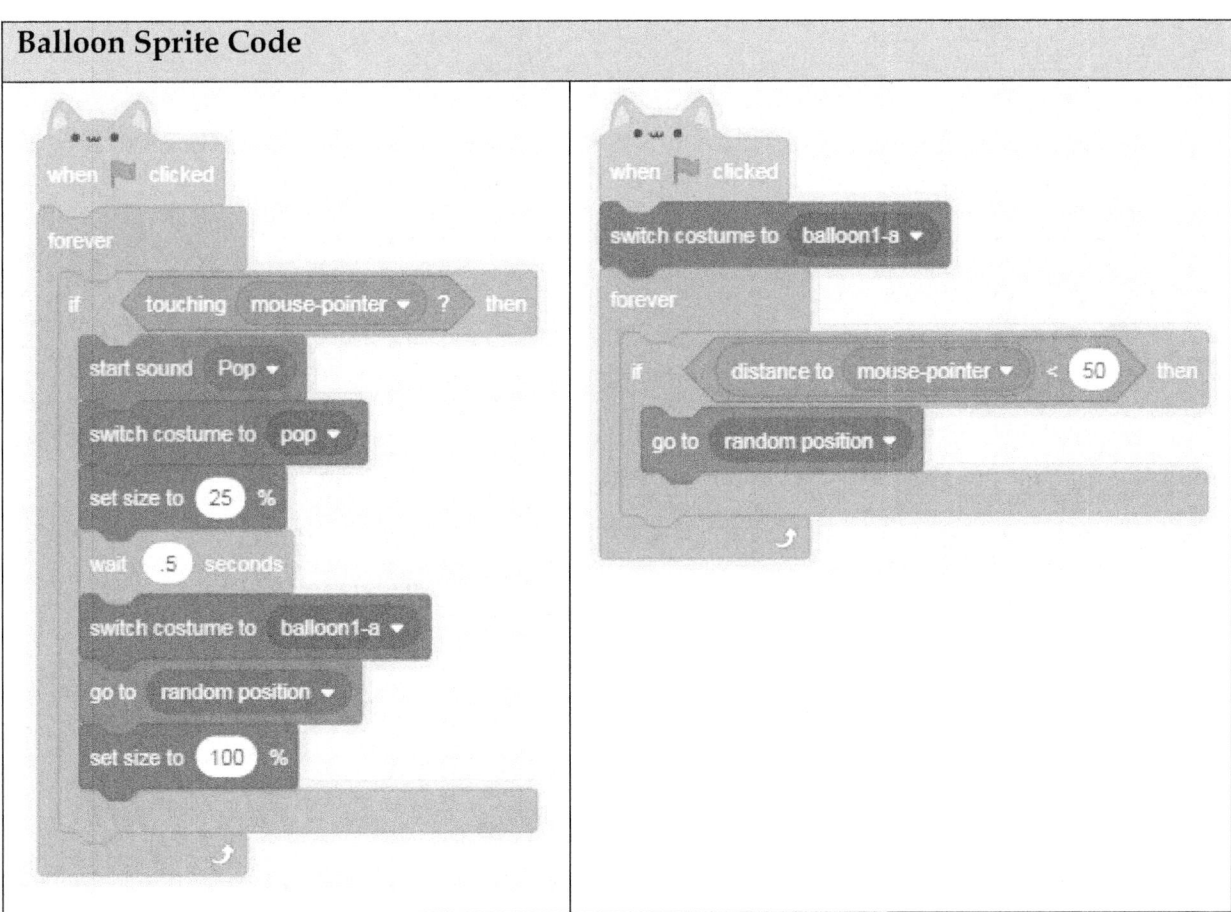

Chapter-8: Balloon Bursting with Finger

In the last chapter, we created a game where with the help of a mouse you can burst balloons with a popping sound effect. In this chapter, we will use the same sprite, background, and almost the same code, but we will be using your webcam for bursting balloons. To execute this code, you must have a working webcam.

Video Sensing

This project will be requiring a video sensing feature for execution. There will be a balloon and on bursting it will produce a pop sound and will get reappear at a different location. The only difference from the last game we made is that for bursting of the balloon instead of a mouse cursor, motion detected from your webcam will be used. You can wave your hand or finger to burst a balloon.

 I have already shared the game on scratch. You can access the game from below QR code or you can use the link given below
https://scratch.mit.edu/projects/510165437/

In scratch, we have an extension to support video sensing. These extensions can be accessed by clicking add extension button at the bottom left corner as shown in the image below:

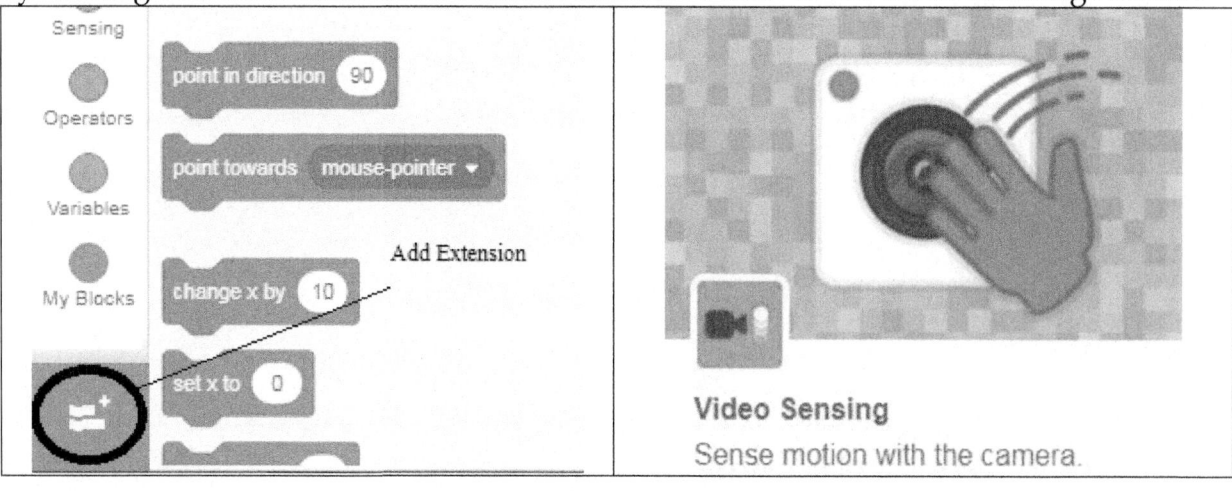

After clicking the "Add Extension" button various additional extensions will appear on a page, from here you can select the Video Sensing extension by clicking it. This will add an extension to the existing panel of the block of codes. Following additional codes will appear on your screen.

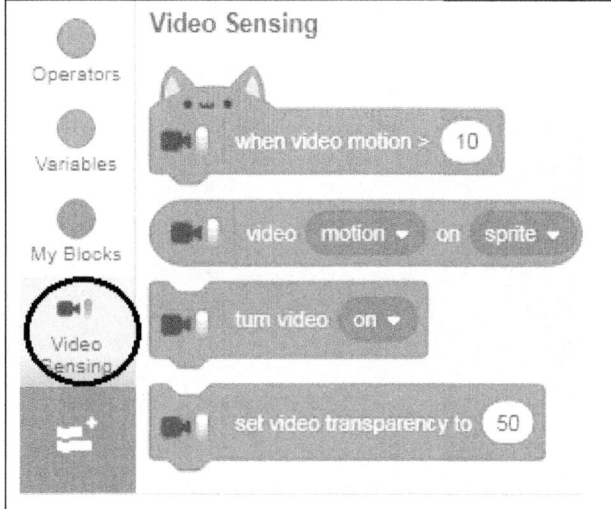

Only 4 code blocks are provided by video sensing. I will explain each one to you one by one.

Video sensors can only measure how fast an object is moving before it. It can therefore act as a good proximity sensor. i.e. a type of sensors normally used in toilet taps etc which can detect hand movement below the tap and can run water. Proximity sensors are also used on doors to automatically open them when someone comes in front of them.

These types of sensors are also used on lift doors, in bulger alarms. In an office or common area, proximity sensors are used to switch off lights after inactivity for a certain duration and turning on the lights after observing any activity.

Similarly, video sensing can provide us with values ranging from 0 to 100. A lower value means low activity observed by webcam and a higher value means a high activity on webcam.

A code block when video motion > 10 can be used to start a video activity-related block on observing activity on a webcam. Another code block is "video motion on sprite", this gives a value of video activity as a number ranging from 0 to 100. If any motion over the sprite is measured, this value increases else remain zero or below 10. The third code of block is fairly simple, it allows us to on/off webcam.

The fourth code of block is "set video transparency to ". Your image from the webcam will be visible in place of the background if the value is set to zero. The complete background will be visible if the value is set to 100. In case the value is set in between, partly background and partly your image will be displayed on the video screen.

Based on the video sensing capabilities we can modify the last game to remove the mouse cursor for the popping of the balloon to use motion to pop the balloons.

The Code

We will remove the code of mouse cursor touching balloon code and instead will place code when video motion on the sprite is greater than some value. A lower value will make the animation more sensitive towards video and a higher value will make it less sensitive to small movements against the webcam.

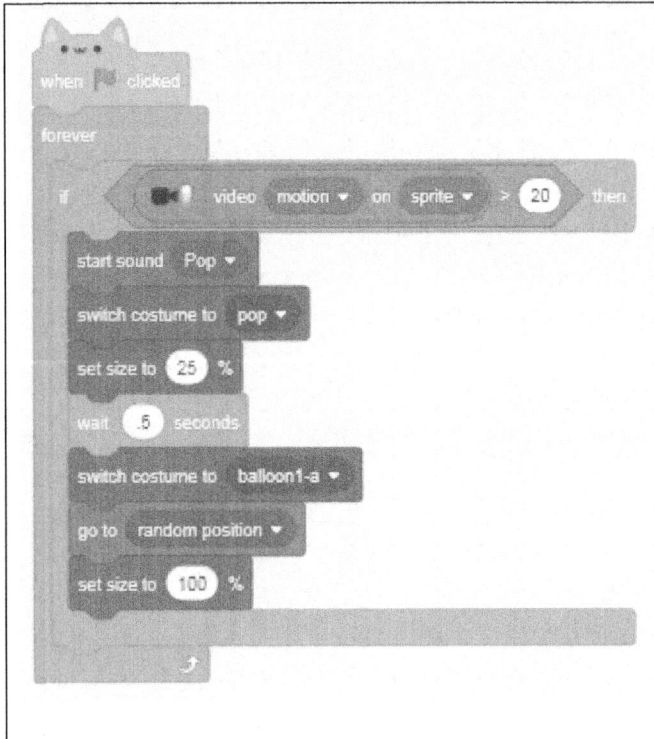

When the system starts, a forever loop will run to check the video motion over the sprite.

If the video moves on the sprite are greater than 20, the code after if block will get executed else nothing will happen.

The rest of the code to change costume and size change have already been discussed in the last chapter so the same is not being discussed here again.

This code block is sufficient to run the game. Run the animation and try to move your hand before the webcam.

Your image blended with the background image will appear as the background to the sprite balloon.

On slow waving of a hand, nothing will happen, however, if you wave your hand faster the balloon will get pop and a fresh balloon will appear at some other location.

This can also be improved by setting the transparency of video as zero, making transparency zero will make the background disappear and your image will become clear on the animation window.

I have observed one issue that even after clicking the stop button of the animation window, the webcam/camera remains on. There is a requirement to off the camera after you have played the fun game. For putting the camera on-off, another set of code has been prepared which stops the camera and all sprites after pressing the space bar.

The entire code is presented here for your ready reference

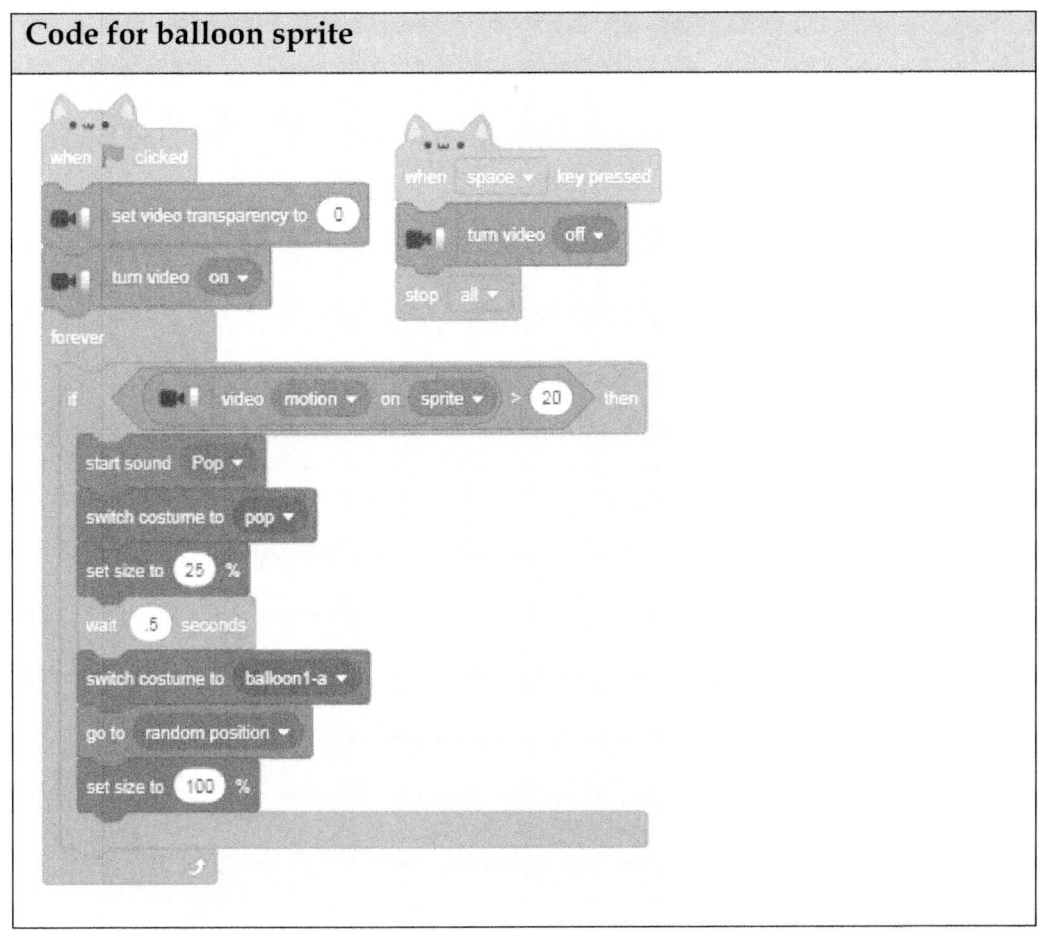

Chapter-9: Rocket Shooting Game (Medium Toughness)

This game has a medium level of toughness, however, if you make the game step by step and include one functionality at a time, you can make it even better.

	The complete game can be accessed by scanning the QR code provided at left or you can directly access the game through this link **https://scratch.mit.edu/projects/511044715/**

The game has a magic wand that produces lightning once you click your mouse. Rockets would come from the top of the screen and you have to aim and shoot the rocket as they are falling. If you shoot it correctly, you get 1 point, if you fail and the rocket reaches the bottom of the screen, you lose one life out of the total 3 lives (chances) provided to you.

As you proceed in the game and your score increases to 5, the speed of the rocket would get doubled. Once you reach the score of 15, the rocket will make a left or right move to avoid your aim. In nutshell, this game increases the toughness level for the player after they score some points. You can add further toughness levels according to your requirement. You may use additional sprites like bombs that can damage your wand and so on.

Now, we will proceed to make this game in phases i.e sprite by sprite by breaking the activities of each sprite into smaller tasks and arranging them in sequence.

Step 1: Make wand moving

Under the step, we would make the wand sprite move according to the movement of the mouse pointer. The wend should move left and right and should not move up and down.

For this purpose, we will import a wand sprite and a background from the scratch library. You can choose any of the images from backgrounds in the library that you like.

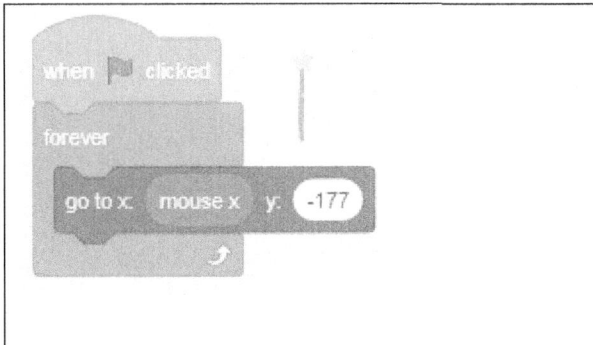

Drag wand sprite to the bottom of the screen like the one in the image. We have to let the wand move with the mouse in the left or right direction, so we will only move the "x-position" of the wand.

Note the "y-position" of the wand from the sprite window. In my case, it is -177. Now we will complete the code.

When the flag button is clicked for the first time, the above code blocks start a forever loop. This loop will every time i.e. with every second or millisecond in time will execute the statement "goto x: mouse x y:-177" block code which is in between the arms of the "forever" code block.

The "x-position" of the mouse and "x-position" of the wand will become equal and with a movement of the mouse, the wand will move. However, note that we have fixed y as -177, the position that we got from the sprite window after dragging and setting it for the first time. With any movement of the mouse, the "y-position" of the sprite will not change i.e. it cannot move up or down in the animation window.

Save the code and run it to check the progress made so far.

In case you have a problem in creating block code "goto x: mouse x y:-177", you can follow the instruction as given below:

1. Take goto x ____ y: ___ code block from motion category of blocks.
2. Type -177 against y
3. Under sensing collection of blocks look for an oval-shaped "mouse x" code block. Drag it and put it over the oval box next to x.

Step 2: Shooting the lightning

The lightning sprite is available in the sprite library. The following are typical features of lightning.

1. It is not on screen when the game starts and till we press a mouse button
2. It appears on the mouse-down button at the location of the wand or mouse's "x-position".
3. It starts moving upward as soon as it appears.
4. It disappears on reaching the other end of the edge.

We will code each one of the statements one by one.

Before we start we need to import the lightning sprite from the sprite library.

	The sprite imported from the library is having a downward direction. Further, in the sprite window, it is showing me direction as 90 degrees. This is not a workable direction of sprite, we need to change the direction of the sprite. Further, the size of the sprite is also very large as compared to our screen size. We can solve these problems either by using code or by customizing sprite using the sprite's editor window.
	Under the sprite window, click on the size and reduce the size. I have made it to 40. Secondly, click on the direction and move the direction arrow till you get your desired direction. We are done!

In case you want to code this, use "set the size to " block from looks and "point in direction" block from motion. Set size to 40 and direction to -90 from the sprite window as shown above.

You can also edit your sprite in the sprite editor, you can drag the sprite to the desired direction in the sprite window and also reduce the size. In all, we have three methods to correct the direction and size of the sprite.

Now, we come to the coding part.

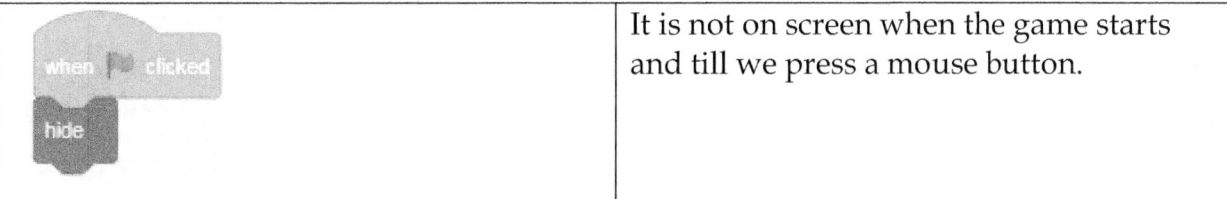	It is not on screen when the game starts and till we press a mouse button.

As per the first feature, this sprite should not be visible on starting of the game. For this, we should add a "hide" code of block from the looks category after when the flag is clicked block. As soon as the flag is clicked, the code hide will be executed in no time and it will disappear from the screen.

You can try the code made till this point to check the progress.

Now, the second feature is to be visible on mouse click.

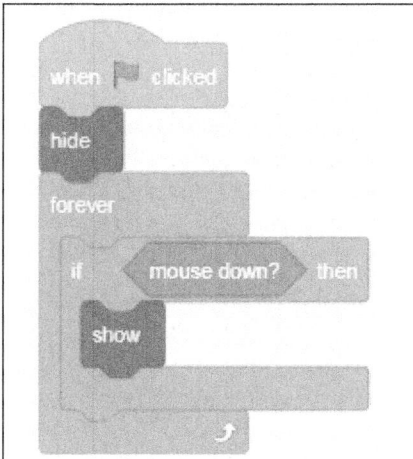	A mouse click is an event, it can happen anytime. The computer should always remain attentive to notice a mouse click, therefore the computer needs to be instructed to look for this event continuously. This can only happen with a forever block of code. After adding forever code of block from "control" set of blocks. We need to ask from animation, whether the mouse-down has occurred? We know that for asking any question to the computer and to receive a yes/no reply, we would require an "if..then" block of code. Drag an "if ...else" block of code and add it below the forever block.

Under the "sensing" blocks of code, we have a "mouse-down" block. If mouse down happens the answer will be "yes" else the answer will be "no". In the case of the "yes" answer, the code between the arms of the "if..then" block will get executed. Now, we would add a "show" block of code from the "looks" blocks of code below it. This will make the lightning sprite visible whenever a mouse-down button is clicked.

The third feature of lightning is that it moves upward on being mouse down.

(code blocks image: when flag clicked, hide, forever, if mouse down? then, show, go to x: mouse x y: -140, repeat 60, move 10 steps)	This means that the code for movement has to come after a mouse-down event has happened. So we should add the next code block under the mouse-down block below the "show" block of code.
	We have already reduced the size and set the direction. We now first need to move lightning to the location of the wand when a click is pressed.
	You can use the goto statement and set it to x = mouse x and y =-140.
	The "y" value has been obtained by dragging the lightning over the wand to know the height value (i.e. y value). We already know that the x value of the wand is the value of the "mouse x" position.
	We will now repeat the "move 10 steps" 30 to 40 times. If you like, move it to 60 times. The purpose is to make lightning reach the other side of the screen edge. What if instead of move 10 steps in a repeat block, I put it like move 400 steps in a single code?

If a single code block to move 400 steps is used, the lightning will move so fast that it will only be visible on the other end.

We can now run the code to check the process of our code and for any possible error(s) in the movement of lightning. What error do you observe?

If the lightning is moving in the left/right direction instead of going straight up. What could be the possible reason for the error? Look at the direction that you have set in the direction window of the sprite. The direction is -90, therefore the sprite is moving in this direction.

To solve this problem, the only possible solution that I find is to edit the sprite in the sprite editor and rotate the sprite in our desired direction such that the direction value is zero.

Let's see how this can be done.

1. Make direction zero in the sprite window
2. Click the sprite and now go to its costume section.
3. Convert the image in a bitmap by clicking the button provided below the image.

4. Use the cursor tool to select the entire image by making a box around it.
5. Now find the rotate sign and rotate the sprite.
6. While rotating keep a watch on the animation window.
7. Rotate till the direction of lightning is in the desired direction in the animation window.

In my case, after rotating the sprite in the editor window, the direction of the sprite in the animation window was upward, however, the direction in the sprite editor window was horizontal. It's ok.

Now, again run the code and the lighting should now go in the desired direction.

Now the only problem, I can notice is that lightning is not disappearing at the top edge of the screen. This problem can be solved by putting a "hide" code below the repeat block.

Now, we have coded all the parts of lightning. It is appearing on click and moving to other edge and getting disappear on reaching another edge. Now, let's code the other sprite i.e. rocket.

Step 3: Moving the rocket

Most of the code for this game would be written under this sprite. As described in earlier sections. The image can be downloaded from google image by searching the rocket keyword. Make sure that the image you select for download is transparent and you save it as a png file and not as jpeg/jpg, BMP, gif, or any other format.

Upload the selected transparent rocket image as a sprite rocket. The main feature of this sprite is that

1. It appears from the top edge of the screen and goes straight down to the bottom edge
2. It appears at any random place at the top edge. Random means a location that is not fixed.
3. After disappearing at the bottom edge it again reappears from the top edge.

Based on the image size and direction, you may have to make necessary adjustments to the sprite by editing the same in the sprite editor window.

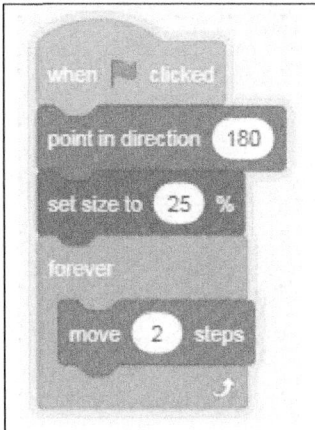

In my case, I have changed direction to 180 degrees and size to 25% as soon as the game starts.

Now for forever, the movement will be 2 steps. This will give slow movement to the rocket sprite.

A feature of the rocket is to get disappear at the other edge and reappearance from the top edge from a random location.

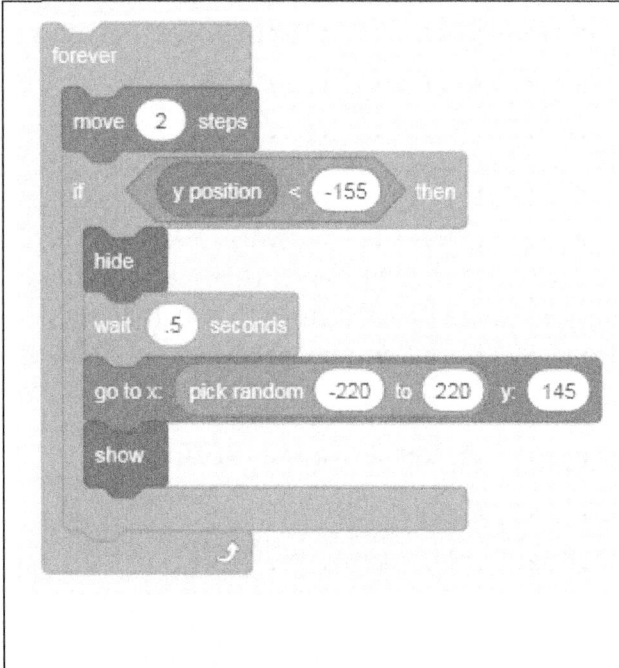

We now need to ask a question from animation, whether the sprite is touching the bottom edge. The answer to this question will be "yes" or "no. So, I will use the "If..then" block.

I will use the "if..then" block under the forever loop so that the animation continuously keeps on looking for this condition.

Now, what is the bottom edge? Drag your rocket sprite to the bottom of the screen from where you want to make it disappear. Note the value of the y position from the sprite window. In my case, it is -155.

If the "y" position of the sprite (can be found in the "motion" set of blocks) is less than -155, it means it is at the bottom edge. We can now add a "hide" block of code (from the looks category of blocks). Before it reappears, I want to wait for 0.5 seconds so that player is ready for the next rocket.

Now, to make the rocket reappear from the top, you need to know what is top of the screen? Just drag the rocket sprite at the top of the screen from where you want the rocket to reappear. Note the "y" position value from the sprite window. In my case, it is 145. To send the rocket to the top location we can use the "goto" block of code from the motion category. Now we know the height from where the rocket will reappear and it is y=145.

We want the rocket to appear from a random location of x from the top. For this purpose, under the operator set of code, we select a "pick random ___ to ____" block. You can measure the width of the screen by dragging and putting sprite at the extreme left and the extreme right position of the animation screen. We have also studied in the earlier section that the center of the screen is 0 and left position is approx.-225 and the right position is approx. +225. If we set the x value of sprite as pick random -225 to 225, this code of block will select any value of x from the range provided.

Now, we will make the sprite visible by using the "show" code of block from the "looks" category of codes.

Now run the animation to check the progress. If the sprite is not moving in the desired direction, check the direction of the sprite and try to edit the same in the sprite editor window to correct the problem.

Step 4: A Blast on being hit

You can observe that on the rocket being hit by lightning, a blast image appears. We need to have that image for our animation. As described in earlier sections. The image can be downloaded from google image by searching the blast keyword. Make sure that the image you select for download is transparent and you save it as a png file and not as jpeg/jpg, BMP, gif, or any other format.

Make another costume of the rocket by uploading the selected transparent blast image. If required use the size button and sprite/costume editor tool to set the correct direction of the "blast" image.

The blast is now the costume of Rocket. If a change costume is executed, the rocket image will change in the "blast" image. The blast will only happen when the rocket sprite touches the lightning sprite.

To know, whether the sprites have touched each other, we have to ask a question from animation. For asking questions from animation having answers in yes and no, we should use the "if-then" block of statement.

Further, we don't know when the two sprites will touch each other. So we have to keep looking for this continuously for the event when two sprites will touch each other. For this purpose, we would put the code blocks in a "forever" loop also use a forever loop.

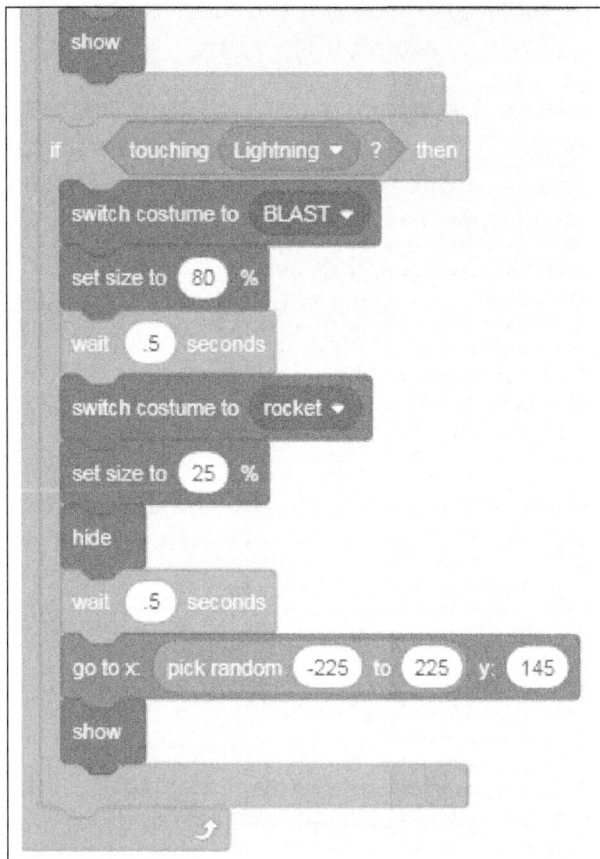	The touching code block can be found in the "sensing" set of codes. Use the drop-down to select lightning.
	On a rocket being touched by lightning, the costume of the rocket will change to blast, The blast costume should remain visible for a while before disappearing. So we have code to switch costume, set size and wait and hide.
	The blast should become rocket and now should reappear from the top, so we will again switch costume and reset the size and got random top location and sprite is made visible.

Step 5: Counting Score

We have already added a counting score code in the last game. Again, we can create a new variable from the variable category of block codes. If you select the variable score, it will become visible in the animation window.

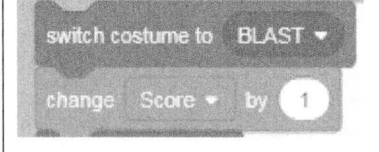	Add a code to increase the score by 1 after the blast happens. We can therefore add the score counting code after the sprite rocket changes its costume to blast.

On each run of the game, the score value continues from the value where you left it in the previous game. This problem can be solved by initializing the value of the score variable to zero on the first run of the game. i.e. we should set score =0 after the flag is clicked.

Step 6: Counting Life

The game provides three chances for a player to play after the player has failed to shoot the rocket and the rocket reaches another side of the screen. Here, I am calling it life, you can call them game or chance or any name as you wish. We have to since, keep track of the "life", we have to create a new variable to store this information. We can create new variable life, in a way similar to the score. If the variable is check marked, it will be visible on the animation window. You can drag the location of life variable location on the animation screen.

The player would lose the game if the rocket reaches the other side of the edge. On the first run of the game i.e. after the flag is clicked, we should set variable life = 3. After the code where the rocket disappears from the bottom edge, we should add a code block to decrease the "life" value by 1.

Here is the code for your ready reference:

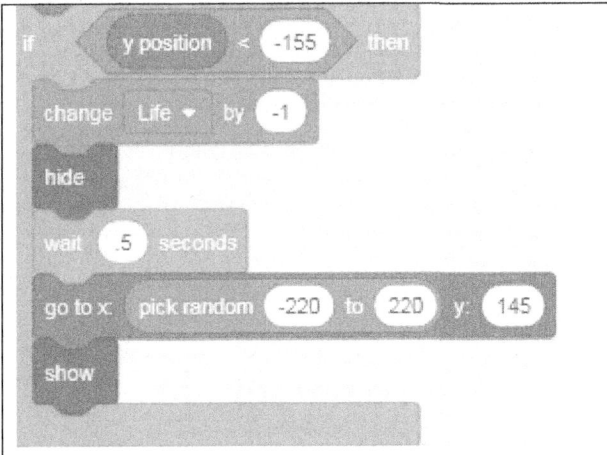	Only an additional block of code "change life by -1" has been inserted just after the condition that confirms that the rocket has reached the bottom edge.

Now, run the code and you will notice that after the rocket reaches another side of the screen, the "life" value reduces by 1. However, after reaching life value zero nothing happens and the game continues. We now need another block of code to let execute the game till life is more than 0 and stop all sprites once life is zero. This can be achieved by the "if..then…else" code block.

	We can place this block such that the game continuation code is put under the "if..then" block and code block to stop all sprites are put under the "else" block of code. We may also need to set the value of life = 3 on the first run, i.e. after the flag button is clicked.

Step 7: Difficulty Level: Increase Speed

All difficulty levels are triggered when a player reaches a particular score. In this case, it is set to score 5.

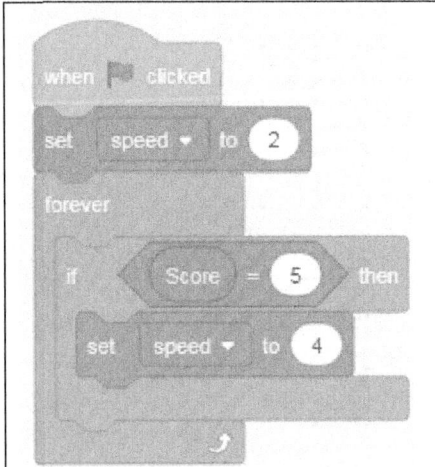	A new variable speed is defined from the "variable" set of blocks. Speed is set to 2 on the first run i.e. after the flag is clicked. Further, the rocket code to "move 2 steps" is also modified to "move speed step".
	Now under a forever loop, the condition for score = 5 is checked, if the condition is found true, the speed variable is set to 4. This will enhance the speed of the rocket after a player scores five points.

Step 8: Difficulty Level: Rocket movement to avoid the aim

The other difficulty level is set when the score is more than 15. This allows the sprite rocket to move in the "x –position" randomly.

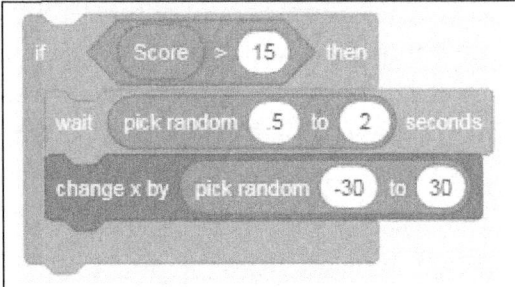	This difficulty level is implemented after checking score condition > 15 under the forever loop.

	If the condition is found true. We will wait for a time between half to 2 seconds. This has been done so that every time the movement in the x-direction is random and the "x-position" is changed from -30 to 30. This can thus be either on the left or right side of the rocket.

If you like, you can improve upon the code by changing sprites or the difficulty level of the game.

I hope that the code I understandable to you. The entire set of the code block is provided on the next page for your study.

The complete code

Lightning Sprite Code	Wand SpriteCode

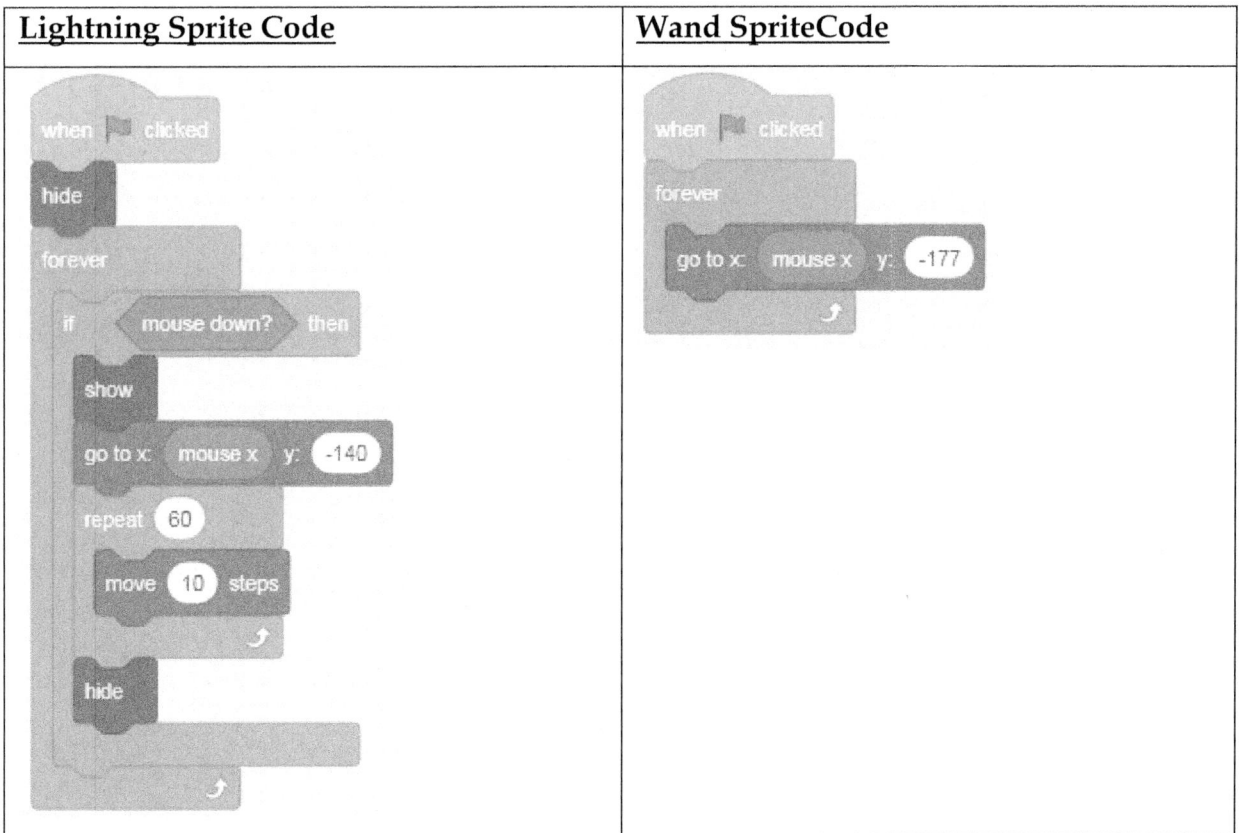

Code 2 for Rocket

```
when [flag] clicked
set speed ▼ to (2)
forever
    if <Score = (5)> then
        set speed ▼ to (4)
```

```
if <Score > (15)> then
    wait (pick random (.5) to (2)) seconds
    change x by (pick random (-30) to (30))
```

Code 1 for rocket sprite

```
when [flag] clicked
point in direction (180)
set size to (25) %
go to x: (0) y: (146)
set Score ▼ to (0)
set Life ▼ to (3)
switch costume to rocket ▼
forever
    if <Life > (0)> then
        move (speed) steps
        if <y position < (-155)> then
            change Life ▼ by (-1)
            hide
            wait (.5) seconds
            go to x: (pick random (-220) to (220)) y: (145)
            show
```

```
if <touching Lightning ▼ ?> then
    switch costume to BLAST ▼
    change Score ▼ by (1)
    set size to (80) %
    wait (.5) seconds
    switch costume to rocket ▼
    set size to (25) %
    hide
    wait (.5) seconds
    go to x: (pick random (-225) to (225)) y: (145)
    show
else
    stop all ▼
```

Chapter 10: Text to speech

The text to speech is an extension that can be added to the scratch platform to add voices for your sprites. It can be added using the extension icon located at the left bottom corner of the scratch editor.

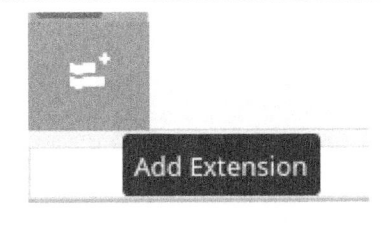	Just click the icon to add the extension and you will be presented with many extensions. From the list of extensions click on the text to speech.
	This will add some more blocks to your block tools. To run text to speech, you would require an internet connection on your computer. If you have the internet on your computer, you will be able to use this extension.

Exploring code blocks for text to speech

The following are three blocks that will appear under the category of text to speech.

speak hello	This is the text-to-speech block. Any word you type in this speak block will be spoken by the computer. You can make language selection and voice selection through the other two modules.
set voice to alto	It supports five different voices some are male voices and some are female voices. You can select anyone for your sprite.

	It supports many languages like french, german, Chinese, and many others. For all practical purposes, you can assume all languages are supported.

Implementation of text to speech

This is very simple and looking to the limitation of the print book where I cannot include output generated from the text to speech, I am keeping it short.

You can include set voice and set the language for initialization before your sprite is instructed to speak anything.

Here in the below example, we will ask our cat sprite to speak "Give me milk, I am hungry"

	The code on left will speak the above sentence on clicking the flag button. We have set voice as alto and language as English. You can change voice and language to explore the code. The only drawback that, I feel this extension lack is the ability to control the speed of the reader.

You can use this extension to create your talking animation or cartoon series.

Solutions to Assignments

Chapter 3: Solutions to Assignments

1. Draw Triangle with each side 100 steps and each angle as 60 degrees (please note the sum of all angles of a triangle is always 180 degree)

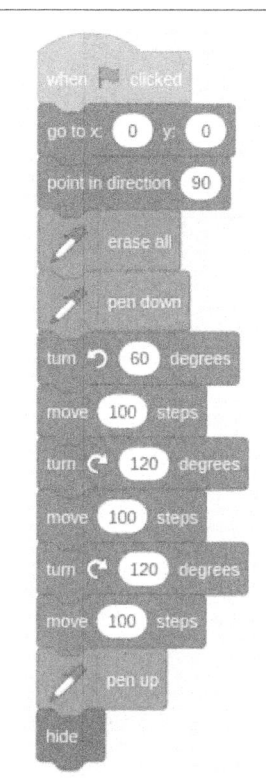	The question is to draw a triangle with each angle as 60 degrees. This is a special type of triangle known as equilateral triangle wherein all sides are equal and each internal angle is 60 degrees. In case anyone side is not equal to the other sides all angles will not be equal. We have used another property of the triangle and used the external angle of 120 degrees for the completion of the triangle. Read the chapter on triangles for complete understanding.

2. Draw a staircase with 10 steps. Each step will have a height of 20 steps and a length of 20 steps.

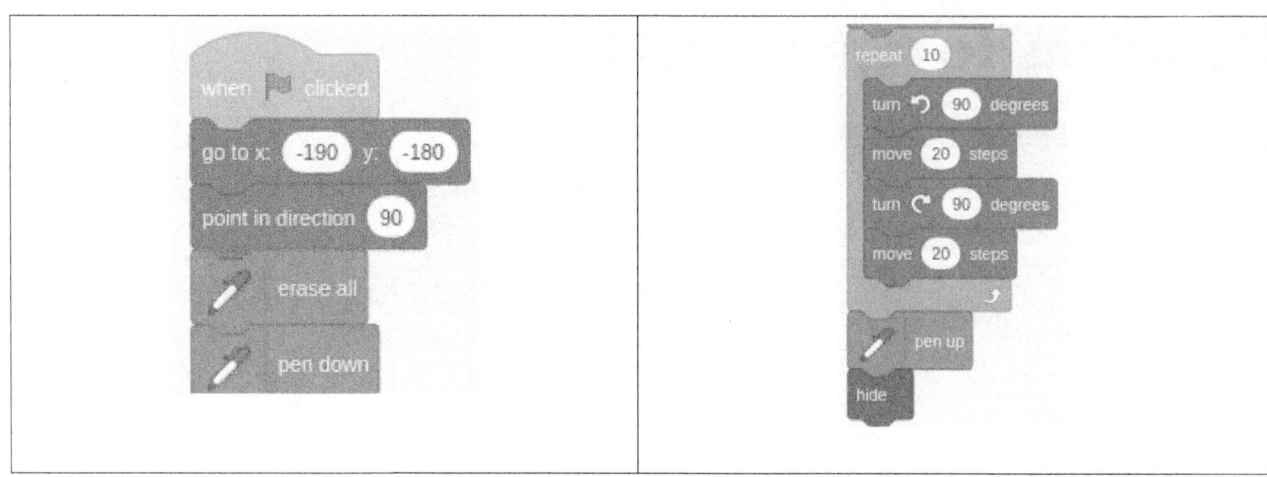

Printed in Great Britain
by Amazon